Sew-It-Yourself
Home Accessories

21 Practical Projects to Make in a Weekend

Cheryl Owen

IMM **lifestyle** ⁘ **books**™

Read. Learn. Do What You Love.

Published 2018--IMM Lifestyle Books
www.IMMLifestyleBooks.com

IMM Lifestyle Books are distributed in the UK by Grantham Book Service, Trent Road, Grantham, Lincolnshire, NG31 7XQ.

In North America, IMM Lifestyle Books are distributed by Fox Chapel Publishing, 903 Square Street, Mount Joy, PA 17552, www.FoxChapelPublishing.com

All photography by Paul Bricknell (Paul Bricknell Photography Ltd) except as follows. Mark Winwood: page 2, 6, 10, 11, 12, 13, 14, 15 top right and bottom right. Africa Studio (Shutterstock): page 3. Manfredxy (Shutterstock): page 5 bottom right. Kostikova Natalia (Shutterstock): page 7. Nitr (Shutterstock): page 15 bottom left.

ISBN 978-1-5048-0093-8

Library of Congress Cataloging-in-Publication Data

Names: Owen, Cheryl, author.
Title: Sew-it-yourself home accessories / Cheryl Owen.
Description: Mount Joy, PA : IMM Lifestyle Books, [2018] | Includes index.
Identifiers: LCCN 2017044254 | ISBN 9781504800938 (pbk.)
Subjects: LCSH: House furnishings. | Machine sewing.
Classification: LCC TT387 .O94 2018 | DDC 646.2/1--dc23
LC record available at https://lccn.loc.gov/2017044254

We are always looking for talented authors. To submit an idea, please send a brief inquiry to acquisitions@foxchapelpublishing.com.

Printed in Singapore
10 9 8 7 6 5 4 3 2 1

Introduction

It's easy to be enticed by the fabulous array of cotton fabrics available today for sewing projects. This book shows you how to turn these fabrics into beautiful home accessories, whether you plan to keep them for yourself or give them as presents. All the projects in this book use small amounts of fabric, so if you already have a glorious stash, you'll find lots of ways to use it! Don't be nervous about mixing prints—it's a great way to use up small pieces of fabric and to give your creations a quirky touch. If you want to use coordinating fabrics, buying a set of fat quarters is a great way of making sure that your fabrics will go well together. Fat quarters are sets of rectangular fabric pieces about 22" x 18" (56 x 45cm) in size. They provide a handy amount of fabric for sewing many small home accessories.

In this book, you will find projects for those new to sewing and for the accomplished sewer. Many projects incorporate techniques that you may not have tried before, such as embroidery or quilting, so it's an ideal way learn something new or to incorporate a familiar, favorite technique. Basic sewing techniques are explained concisely at the beginning of the book, and each project has clear instructions and step-by-step photography to guide you and give you confidence as you work. Even if you are already an experienced sewer, there are lots of innovative ideas and suggestions included here that will inspire you to create projects with your own flair. Enjoy filling your home with this variety of home accessories!

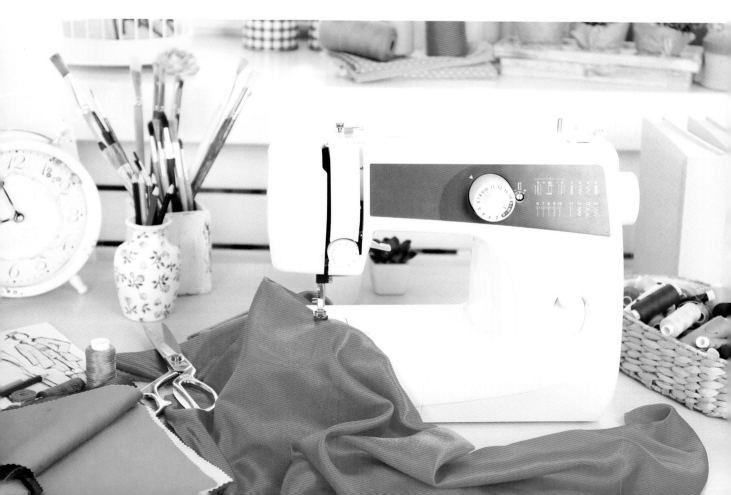

Contents

Materials, Supplies, and Tools

Materials

Your main fabric is not the only material you might need when sewing! From interfacing to batting (wadding), there are several other materials you might need in addition to your fabric of choice.

Cotton Fabric

All the projects in this book are made from cotton. It is the easiest of fabrics to work with, so it's just right for a beginner. The variety of printed cotton fabric is vast, inexpensive, and widely available. Check your local fabric store or shop online. Many cotton fabrics are produced for patchwork and quilting purposes, and it's these kinds of fabrics that have been used for most of the projects in this book. You can easily complement the prints by using coordinating, pattern-free cottons. Heavier-weight cottons are suitable for simple cushions, aprons, and bags (such as the tote bag on page 86). Most printed fabrics have a right and wrong side, and it's usually quite obvious which is the right side. Most plain fabrics, woven stripes, and woven checkered fabrics do not have a wrong side; these are known as double-faced fabrics.

As it is a natural fiber, cotton may shrink. To test for shrinkage, cut a 4" x 4" (10 x 10cm) square of fabric. Wash and press the square, then measure it again. If the square is now smaller than 4" x 4" (10 x 10cm), it has shrunk, and you should wash your fabric before cutting out the pieces for the project.

Interfacing

Stiffen fabric with interfacing to give it more body or to add strength. Nonwoven and woven varieties of interfacing come in different weights to suit particular purposes. Interfacing is sold in packs or by the yard (meter). Iron the shiny side of iron-on (fusible) interfacing, or baste (tack) sew-in interfacing to the wrong side of the fabric.

Fusible (bonding) web, which is similar to interfacing, is a double-sided adhesive web with a paper backing that is used to fuse layers of fabric together.

Batting (Wadding)

A layer of batting (wadding) is sandwiched between fabrics to pad them. It comes in various weights and is made from man-made fibers such as polyester or natural fibers such as cotton, wool, and eco-friendly bamboo. Use cotton batting (wadding) for items that will come in contact with heat. Batting (wadding) made from natural fibers is prone to shrink, whereas polyester isn't, so if you are planning to wash an item frequently, it might be more practical to use polyester instead of cotton.

Use a layer of insulated lining in items that will come into contact with heat (such as the pot holder on page 68 or the oven mitt on page 34). It reflects warmth back to the body and is breathable, letting moisture escape. Just remember: insulated lining is heat resistant but not heat proof.

Supplies

Find a nice selection of supplies at department stores and sewing shops. Don't be afraid to collect a large stash of buttons, ribbons, and other trimmings—they will come in handy for lots of applications!

Threads

For machine and hand sewing, choose sewing thread to match the fabric colors of your project. The thread should be strong and durable with a bit of give in it; an all-purpose polyester thread is a good choice, and it has more give in it than an all-purpose cotton thread.

Topstitching is machine stitching on the right side of the fabric, both for decoration and to hold fabric layers in place. Topstitched projects in this book use regular sewing thread, but you can also find thick topstitching thread in a small range of colors. Use thick topstitching thread with a topstitching needle and ordinary sewing thread in the bobbin.

Embroidery floss (stranded cotton) is a versatile embroidery thread made up of six strands that can be separated for use in any quantity desired (1 strand to 6 strands), which allows you to precisely control the thickness of your embroidery lines. It's inexpensive and comes in a huge variety of colors.

Buttons

Use buttons for practical purposes as well as for decoration. As you can imagine, there is a huge variety available out there, in every shape and color. Flat buttons have flat backs with two or four holes to sew through. Shank buttons have a loop underneath to sew through. Self-cover buttons allow you to cover the button with a fabric of your choice; they are available in different sizes and are easy to assemble, so rest assured if you want the buttons on a project to match perfectly, you can do that!

Ribbons

Use ribbons for decoration or for fastenings. They come in various widths and finishes and in lots of colors.

Cotton Twill Tape

Usually a utility tape for binding edges or reinforcing seams, cotton twill tape comes in a small range of widths and colors. It is cheap to buy and, in this book, is perfect for making apron ties (see the half apron on page 26).

Zippers

For a professional finish on a bag or other item, close two edges of fabric temporarily with a zipper. It's easiest to stitch a zipper with a zipper foot on a sewing machine.

Bias Binding

This is a strip of bias cut fabric (see page 13) with the long edges pressed under for binding curved and straight edges. The binding is available in different widths and a limited color range, plus a small choice of printed bindings. Buy bias binding by the yard (meter) or in packs of 3 yd. (2.5m), or make your own bias binding with a bias binding maker (see page 9).

Metal Hardware

Use round, square, rectangular, and D-shaped metal rings to link straps to bags and to hang items on a wall. A swivel bolt snap is a trigger-style fastener to join a strap or handle and metal ring together, allowing the strap to be removed. A key ring is a split ring that can be affixed securely through the hole in a key. Metal rings and swivel bolt snaps come in different finishes, such as chrome and antique bronze.

Metal eyelets are available in a few different sizes and have nickel, gold, and painted finishes. Most come with an installation kit or are applied with special pliers or a setting tool.

Hook and Loop Tape

This two-part tape, commonly known by the brand name Velcro®, is used to fasten bags and clothing. One tape has a looped mesh surface and the other a hooked surface. The two layers interlock when pressed together. Hook and loop tape can be sewn on or can have a self-adhesive backing for sticking. It is also available as circular disks.

Tools

Even if you are new to sewing, you probably already have some of the basic equipment you'll need to get started. Keep your tools together and use them only for sewing activities; otherwise, they may become blunt and dirty. Keep sharp and swallowable tools beyond the reach of small children and pets.

Pattern-Making Papers

None of the templates in this book need paper larger than 11" x 17" (A3 size), and most only need standard printer paper size. Sewing shops supply special pattern-making paper, but ordinary printer paper is ideal to use. Brown kraft paper (parcel paper) is also suitable as it is durable and comes in large sheets. Thinner tracing paper is useful for making templates you will need to see through, such as for projects where you need to position motifs.

Pattern-Making Tools

Use a sharp #2 (HB) pencil or mechanical pencil for accurate drawing. Draw straight lines against a ruler and draw circles with a compass. Use a triangle ruler (set square) to make precise angles when drawing on paper and fabric.

Measuring Tools

A transparent 12" (30cm) ruler is a handy size for drawing straight lines on paper and fabric and for checking measurements. Use a yardstick (meter stick) for long lengths and to measure fabric quantities. A plastic-coated or cloth measuring tape is useful for measuring curves. A 6" (15cm)-long sewing gauge has a slider to set at different levels for marking hems and seams and to use as a quilting guide.

Fabric-Marking Tools

A sharp #2 (HB) pencil can be used on fabric if the marks will be hidden. Use an air-erasable pen if the marks will be visible; the marks will gradually fade away. Alternatively, use a water-soluble marker, which allows the marks to be removed with water. Tailor's chalk comes in a range of colors and in pencil and wedge form; marks made with tailor's chalk will brush off, although a slight mark may remain. Keep tailor's chalk sharpened for accuracy. Test all methods of marking fabric on scrap fabric first to make sure you'll get what you want.

Scissors

Cut paper with paper scissors, not sewing scissors. Bent-handled dressmaking shears are comfortable and accurate to use for cutting fabric because the angle of the lower blade allows the fabric to lie flat. Top-quality shears are expensive, but they will last a lifetime. The shears are available in different sizes, so test which ones you prefer before buying. A small pair of embroidery scissors is indispensable for snipping threads and seam allowances. Pinking shears cut a fray-resistant zigzag edge for finishing seams and to cut fabrics that are prone to fraying.

Needles

Needle sizes are identified by number. Sewing machine needles come in different thicknesses with points of different shapes. Sizes 9–14 (70–90 in the UK) are the most commonly used (the lower the number, the finer the point). A sharp-point needle is the most versatile for woven fabrics. Use a ballpoint needle on knit fabrics. Replace sewing machine needles regularly, as they soon become blunt and put strain on your sewing machine.

The number system is different for hand-sewing needles: the higher the number, the shorter and finer the needle. Use crewel embroidery needles for embroidery; they have a large eye to accommodate more than one strand and are easy to thread. They are also handy for general sewing; sizes 7–9 are useful sizes.

Pins

Dressmaking pins come in various thicknesses; household pins are the most versatile. Use lace or bridal pins on delicate fabrics, as other pins may mark the surface. Colored glass-headed pins show up well on a large expanse of fabric. Quilting pins are extra long to push through fabric layers, and they have large, colorful, shapely heads to make them easy to see.

Bodkin and Rouleau Turner

A bodkin is a needle-like tool that has a large eye and blunt tip. Fasten a bodkin to the end of a rouleau or other narrow tube of fabric to turn it right side out. Also known as a tube turner, a rouleau turner can be used instead of a bodkin to turn a tube of fabric through. You can also simply use a safety pin instead of a bodkin or rouleau turner, by working it through manually, but it will be a slow process.

Bias Binding Maker

When you pull a bias or a straight strip of fabric through this clever gadget, it will turn under the long edges for you; then you simply press with an iron to make a binding. Bias binding makers come in a range of widths and are a useful tool for a keen sewer.

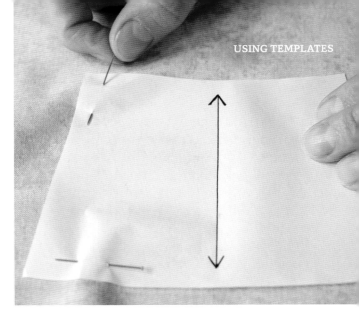

Techniques

The same basic methods are used throughout this book, so read this section before embarking on any projects and try out the techniques on scrap fabric first. When following instructions, it is important to use imperial or metric measurements, but not a combination of both, because some measurements are not exact equivalents but instead rounded to be easy for the reader to use.

Keep a basic sewing toolbox on hand for all projects. This should include a sharp #2 (HB) pencil, an air-erasable fabric pen or water-soluble marker or tailor's chalk, dressmaking shears, embroidery scissors, a ruler, a tape measure, dressmaking pins, a selection of sewing threads, hand-sewing needles, and a bodkin or rouleau turner.

Cutting Out

Many of the projects in this book are made from squares and rectangles and can be drawn directly onto the fabric using a sharp #2 (HB) pencil, an air-erasable fabric pen, a water-soluble marker, or tailor's chalk. For the projects that require other shapes, there are templates on pages 94-103.

Press the fabric before cutting out to remove any wrinkles. Woven fabrics stretch differently if pulled in different directions. The direction the threads are woven is known as the grain. The lengthwise grain, which runs parallel with the selvages, is called the warp. (The selvage is the self-finished edge of a fabric that does not unravel). The warp has less stretch, meaning it is easier to sew parallel to the warp without the fabric stretching or puckering. The grain that runs across the fabric from selvage to selvage is the weft. It has a little more stretch than the warp. Cut rectangles and squares with the edges parallel with the warp and weft.

Using Templates

Photocopy the templates as needed, enlarging them if indicated. Alternatively, trace any actual size templates onto tracing paper, label them correctly, and mark all the fold lines, grain lines, dots, notches, and other details. Cut out the templates with a pair of standard scissors (not your sewing scissors!).

Sewing patterns and templates indicate the grain line with an arrow. When positioning a template, keep the grain line parallel with the fabric selvage or with the grain of the fabric if there is no selvage. Lay the fabric out flat and smooth on a table. To cut pairs of templates, fold the fabric parallel with the selvage to make a double layer. Match the "place on fold" line of the template on the fabric fold and pin the template in place or draw around it. Pin the layers together and cut them out along the drawn outline. Otherwise, keep the fabric flat with no fold.

If you need to cut batting (wadding) or insulated lining on the fold, trace the template onto a sheet of folded tracing paper, matching the "place on fold" line on the fold. Cut out the template and open it out flat. Pin the template to the surface of the batting (wadding) or insulated lining and cut out. Mark the position of any dots on the fabric with a pin or an air-erasable pen. Snip any notches in the seam allowance.

Positioning Motifs

If your fabric has a distinctive motif, you may wish to show it in its entirety, for example, centered on a cushion. Make a template from tracing paper. Mark the seam allowance and grain line. Fold the template into quarters to find the center, then open it out flat again. Lay the template over the motif on the fabric, matching the grain lines and the center of the template to the center of the motif. Pin in place or draw around the template and cut it out. If the fabric is checkered, or has stripes or a repeated print, center these as well so they will be positioned symmetrically. You may need a larger amount of fabric than is called for in the materials list to allow for positioning motifs.

Basting (Tacking)

Basting (tacking) stitches join fabric layers together temporarily. The more you stitch and gain confidence, the less reliant on basting (tacking) you will become. You can baste (tack) by hand or by using a long machine stitch. Basting (tacking) is always useful for tricky areas such as joining many layers of fabric, stitching corners, or stitching tight curves. Work basting (tacking) stitches in a contrasting thread so they are easy to see (and remove later) and baste (tack) just inside the seam allowance so the basting (tacking) stitches are easy to remove once the final seam is stitched. Always remove the basting (tacking) stitches once the seam has been completed, unless advised otherwise.

Seams

Before stitching, match the seam allowances and pin together. You can position pins perpendicular to the seam line, which will allow you to stitch right over them; or you can insert the pins parallel to the seam line and remove them as you stitch. Experiment and see which method you prefer—it could be a combination of both.

A plain seam is the most commonly used seam and occurs throughout these projects. With right sides facing and raw edges of the seam allowances

Stitching

The projects in this book are worked using simple stitches on the sewing machine—mostly straight stitch, but also zigzag stitch to finish raw fabric edges. Occasionally, you will need to stitch by hand, such as when basting (tacking), closing openings, and sewing on buttons.

level, stitch the seam, maintaining the same distance from the raw edges. Sewing machines have lines on the needle plate that are standard seam allowance distances from the needle; keep the raw fabric edges level with the relevant line to keep the size of the seam allowance consistent. Stitch back and forth repeatedly for about ⅜" (1cm) at the start and finish of each seam in order to keep the ends of the seam from unraveling.

Joining a curved edge to a straight edge is a little more difficult. To help the curve lay flat, snip into the curved seam allowance at regular intervals, then pin and stitch the seam.

To topstitch on the right side, stitch parallel with a seam to emphasize it and to hold a seam allowance or fabric layers in place. To accentuate the stitching, use contrasting thread or thick topstitching thread.

Grading (Layering) Seam Allowances

Reduce the bulk of fabric in a seam allowance by trimming each layer of fabric in the seam allowance by different amounts after the seam has been stitched (see the photo at top left).

Finishing (Neatening) Seams

Most seams in home sewing projects will be hidden under another fabric layer or a lining.

Protect raw edges that won't be hidden and will be prone to wear and tear with a zigzag stitch. Set the stitch width to about ⅛" (3mm) wide and ⅛" (3mm) apart, then zigzag stitch along the raw edge. If you prefer, trim the seam with a pair of pinking shears.

Clipping Corners and Snipping Curves

Use embroidery scissors to cut the seam allowance across corners and to carefully snip "V" shapes (notches) into curved seam allowances after the seam has been stitched. This will help the fabric lay flat when it is turned right side out. Take care not to snip the stitching (see the photo at bottom left).

Slipstitching

Slipstitching is used to join two folded edges or one folded edge to a flat surface, such as closing a gap in a seam or to secure binding. Keep the stitches small and work from right to left. With a single thread (unless advised otherwise), bring the needle out through one folded edge. Pick up a few threads of the fabric on the opposite edge and insert the needle back through the folded edge about ¼" (6mm) from where it emerged. Repeat along the length.

LAYERING SEAMS

FINISHING (NEATENING) SEAMS

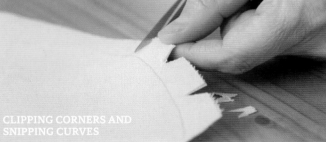
CLIPPING CORNERS AND SNIPPING CURVES

SLIPSTITCHING

Using Bias Strips

Strips cut on the bias can be used to make bias binding and rouleaux. The bias is any direction on the fabric that is not the warp or weft. The bias will stretch, so take care when stitching, or the seam will end up puckered.

Cutting Bias Strips

Fold and press the fabric diagonally at a 45-degree angle to the selvage. This diagonal fold is the true bias. Open and lay the fabric flat again. Using a ruler and a sharp #2 (HB) pencil, an air-erasable pen, or tailor's chalk, draw lines the width of the bias strip required parallel with the pressed line. To make bindings, add 4" (10cm) to the desired length for easing and turning under the ends. Add extra for joins.

Joining Bias Strips

JOINING BIAS STRIPS

Position one end of two strips at right angles, with the right sides facing and matching the raw ends. Stitch the bias strips together, using a ¼" (6mm) seam allowance. Press the seam open and cut off the extending corners.

Bindings

Although ready-made binding is widely available, it is economical and quick to make your own. Curved edges must be bound with bias binding, whereas straight edges can be bound with bias or straight binding. Create single bias or straight binding with a bias binding maker. The manufacturer's instructions will indicate the width to cut the binding; it's usually twice the width of the narrow end of the bias binding maker.

Making Bias Binding

MAKING BIAS BINDING

Push the strip (wrong side up) through the wide end of a bias binding maker. If necessary, poke a pin through the gap in the top of the bias binding maker to ease the binding through. The edges will be turned under as the binding emerges out of the narrow end. Press the binding as you pull it through.

Attaching Single-Fold Binding

1. Open out one folded edge of the binding. Pin the binding to the fabric, either with right sides facing if you wish to finish the binding by hand on the underside, or with the right side of the binding facing the wrong side of the fabric if you want to topstitch the binding on the right side of the item. Stitch along the fold line.
2. Turn the binding over the raw edge. To finish by hand on the underside, match the pressed edge to the seam, pin, and then slipstitch the pressed edge along the seam. To finish by machine, pin the pressed edge just beyond the seam to hide it, pin, and then topstitch close to the pressed edge.

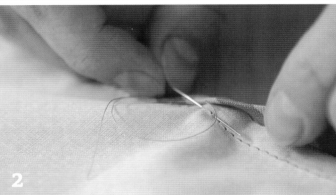

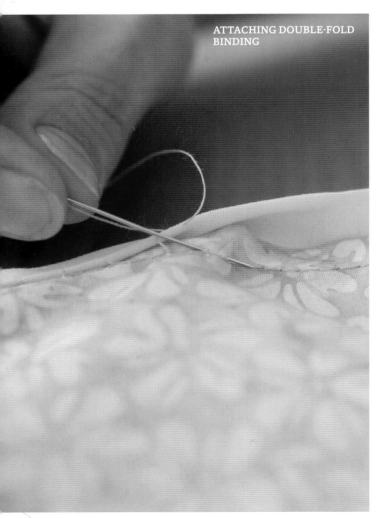

ATTACHING DOUBLE-FOLD BINDING

Attaching Double-Fold Binding

To make double-fold binding from bias or straight strips, press the binding lengthwise in half with wrong sides facing. Matching the raw edges, pin and stitch the binding to the fabric, either with right sides facing if you wish to finish the binding by hand on the underside, or with the right side of the binding facing the wrong side of the fabric if you want to topstitch the binding on the right side of the item. Turn the binding over the raw edge. To finish by hand on the underside, match the pressed edge to the seam, pin, and then slipstitch the pressed edge along the seam. To finish by machine, pin the pressed edge just beyond the seam to hide it, pin, and then topstitch close to the pressed edge.

Rouleaux

A rouleau is a narrow tube of bias cut fabric. Being bias cut, rouleaux bend easily. They have many uses, such as for ties, loops for fastening buttons, and hanging loops for suspending items. When calculating the width to cut, double the required width and add two ¼" (6mm) seam allowances. Add extra to the length for turning in ends or inserting into seams.

1. Cut a bias strip of fabric. Fold lengthwise in half with right sides facing. Stitch the long raw edges, using a ¼" (6mm) seam allowance unless advised otherwise.

2. To turn right side out, fasten a bodkin to one end of the tube with a short length of double thread. Ease the bodkin through the tube, and it will pull the rouleau right side out. Alternatively, slip a rouleau turner into the tube, hook it onto the end of the tube, and pull it through. If the rouleau has wrinkled, steam it with an iron held just above the wrinkles.

Chenille Sofa Pillow

The quilting on this gorgeous cushion has a tactile chenille effect that looks soft and textured. Two layers of fabric are padded with batting (wadding) and stitched in diagonal rows, then the top layer is cut to reveal the fabric underneath. It's an easy trick to achieve a cool look!

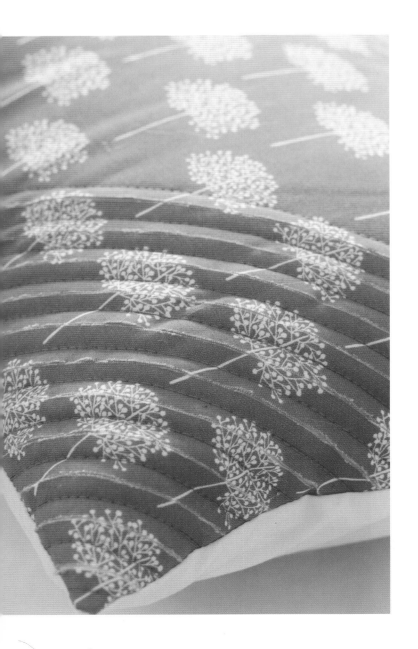

Materials

- 20" x 16" (50 x 40cm) rectangle of printed cotton fabric
- 20" x 16" (50 x 40cm) rectangle of lightweight batting (wadding)
- 20" x 16" (50 x 40cm) rectangle of lightweight white cotton fabric
- 16" (40cm) of 44" (112cm)-wide plain cotton fabric
- 16" x 12" (40 x 30cm) pillow form (cushion pad)

Cutting Out

- Cut one 16¾" x 12¾" (42 x 32cm) rectangle for the front from the printed fabric, batting (wadding), lightweight white fabric, and plain fabric.
- Cut two 12¾" x 11½" (32 x 29cm) rectangles for the backs from the plain fabric.

Making the pillow

1. **Draw parallel lines.** Measure 9" (23cm) from one corner of the printed front along each adjacent edge and mark each edge with a pin. Use a ruler and sharp #2 (HB) pencil to draw a diagonal line between the pins, forming a triangle. Draw multiple parallel lines ½" (1.2cm) apart on the triangle, all the way into the corner. Repeat on the diagonally opposite corner.

2. **Prepare the front.** Place the batting (wadding) on the white fabric, then place the plain fabric on that, then place the printed fabric front, right side up, on top. Smooth the layers out from the center and pin together. Baste (tack) the outer edges.

3. **Stitch the lines.** Stitch along the drawn lines, making sure to stitch back and forth at each end of each line to secure. Take care not to stretch the fabric as you stitch. Remove the basting (tacking) along the edges that have been stitched.

4. **Create the chenille effect.** Slide the lower blade of a pair of sharp embroidery scissors or small sewing scissors between the printed and plain fabric between two rows of stitching. Carefully cut the top printed layer to reveal the plain fabric underneath. Repeat this cut between all the rows of stitching on each corner.

5. **Hem the backs.** Press under ⅜" (1cm), then ¾" (2cm) on one long edge of the back fabric pieces. Stitch close to the inner pressed edges to hem the backs.

6. **Pin the back and front together.** Pin the backs to the front with right sides together, matching the raw edges and overlapping the hems.

7. **Finish the pillow.** Stitch the outer edges, using a ⅜" (1cm) seam allowance. Clip the corners. Turn the pillow cover right side out and insert the pillow form (cushion pad).

Tip

If you'd like to create the chenille technique on other projects, remember to stitch and cut the lines on the bias grain so the cut edges won't fray.

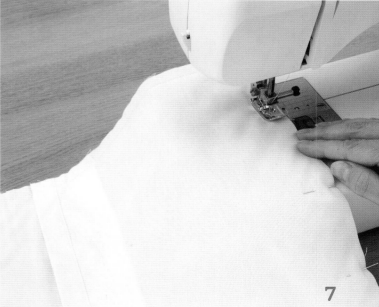

Coffeepot Cozy

Make a padded cozy to pop over a coffeepot to keep its contents hot. This smart cozy has an added bonus, too—a mug-shaped pocket to store coffee spoons or sugar packets. Have fun choosing the contrasting fabric for the pocket!

Materials

- 6" (15cm) of 44" (112cm)-wide printed cotton fabric
- 24" x 12" (60 x 30cm) rectangle of polka dot cotton fabric
- 24" x 12" (60 x 30cm) rectangle of lightweight batting (wadding)
- 24" x 12" (60 x 30cm) rectangle of lightweight white cotton fabric
- 24" x 12" (60 x 30cm) rectangle of plain cotton fabric

Cutting Out

- Find the coffeepot cozy templates on pages 94 and 95.
- Cut two mugs on the fold, one 3½" x 1¼" (9 x 3cm) bias strip for the handle, and one 20" x 2¾" (50 x 7cm) straight strip for the binding from the printed fabric.
- Cut two coffeepot cozies on the fold from the polka dot fabric, batting (wadding), lightweight white fabric, and plain fabric.

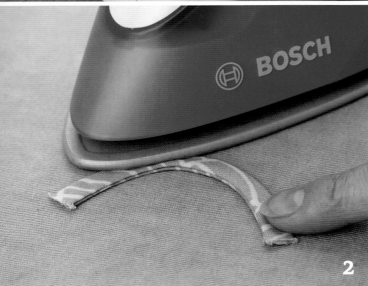

Making the cozy

1. **Make the mug.** With right sides facing and using a ¼" (6mm) seam allowance, pin and stitch the mugs together around the outer edges, leaving a 1½" (4cm) gap in the center of the short lower edge. Clip the corners, snip the curves, and turn the mug right side out. Fold under the seam allowance along the edges of the gap. Press the mug.

2. **Make the mug handle.** Refer to the rouleaux technique (page 15) to make the handle. Press the handle flat in a curved shape with the seam at the inner curve.

3. **Sew on the mug.** Refer to the template to mark the position of the corners of the mug with pins on the right side of one polka dot cozy piece. Pin the mug to the cozy, matching the corners to the pinned marks. Slip the ends of the handle under the right-hand edge of the mug, then pin and baste (tack) the mug and handle in position. Sew the handle to the cozy with small, neat hand stitches. Topstitch close to the edges of the mug, leaving the top edge open and stitching back and forth a few times at the upper edge to reinforce the stitching.

4. **Layer the fabrics.** In two sets, place each batting (wadding) cozy piece on a lightweight fabric cozy piece, then place a polka dot cozy piece right side up on top of that. Smooth the fabrics out from the center and pin the layers together. Baste (tack) around the outer edges.

5. **Stitch the cozy.** Pin the two cozy sets together with right sides facing. Stitch the outer edges, using a ⅜" (1cm) seam allowance and leaving the lower edge open. Snip the curves. Press the seams open with the tip of the iron to avoid

flattening the batting (wadding). Repeat to stitch the plain fabric cozies together for the lining. Turn the polka dot cozy right side out and insert the lining inside, matching the seams and lower raw edges. Baste (tack) the raw edges together.

6. **Bind the lower edge.** Refer to the double-fold binding technique (page 14) to bind the lower edge of the cozy. Use a ⅜" (1cm) seam allowance and fold under ¼" (6mm) at one end of the binding to start, then overlap the ends of the binding. To finish, slipstitch the binding to the lining of the cozy.

Tip

The cozy fits a small coffeepot. Adjust the size for a larger pot by adding an inch (centimeter) or so to the outer edges of the cozy template. Remember to cut the binding longer, too.

Cute Egg Coaster

Join contrasting fabrics to make a set of funky coasters. A layer of insulated lining inside makes them heat resistant, and a single fabric on the underside means they are reversible, too.

Materials
(for one coaster)

- 8" x 5" (20 x 15cm) rectangle of printed cotton fabric
- 5" x 4" (15 x 10cm) rectangle of polka dot cotton fabric
- 5" x 4" (15 x 10cm) rectangle of insulated lining
- 14" (35cm) of ½" (1.2cm)-wide bias binding

Cutting Out

- Find the coaster template on page 96.
- Cut one coaster and one upper egg from printed fabric.
- Cut one lower egg from polka dot fabric.
- Cut one coaster from insulated lining.

Tip

Make a coaster to match the mug hug on page 60! You can simply embroider a squiggly line over the seam on the coaster with a chain stitch.

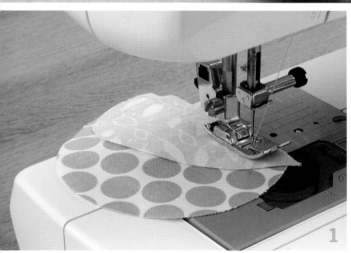

Making the coaster

1. **Assemble the coaster.** Pin and stitch the upper egg to the lower egg along the straight edge with right sides facing, using a ¼" (6mm) seam allowance. Press the seam open. Place the insulted lining coaster on the wrong side of the fabric coaster, then place the stitched coaster right side up on top. Pin and baste (tack) the layers together.

2. **Add the binding.** Open out one end of the binding and fold under ¼" (6mm). Refer to the single-fold binding technique (page 14) to bind the coaster, overlapping the ends of the binding. Finish by slipstitching the binding to the underside of the coaster.

Half Apron

This stylish half apron is a great project for a beginner. It has a generous patch pocket for keeping tools at hand and ties attached to large metal eyelets that will hold up well to frequent wear. The ties are long enough to wrap around and fasten at the front if you want.

Materials

- 28" x 8" (70 x 20cm) rectangle of plain fabric
- 28" x 18" (70 x 45cm) rectangle of printed cotton fabric (fabric A)
- 12" x 10" (30 x 25cm) rectangle of printed cotton fabric (fabric B)
- Two ⅝" (1.5cm) metal eyelets and setting tool
- 2½ yd. (2m) of 1" (2.5cm)-wide cotton twill tape

Cutting Out

- Cut one 26¾" x 6¼" (68 x 16cm) rectangle for the upper apron from plain fabric.
- Cut one 26¾" x 15½" (68 x 39cm) rectangle for the lower apron from printed fabric A.
- Cut one 11" x 8¼" (28 x 21cm) rectangle for the pocket from printed fabric B.

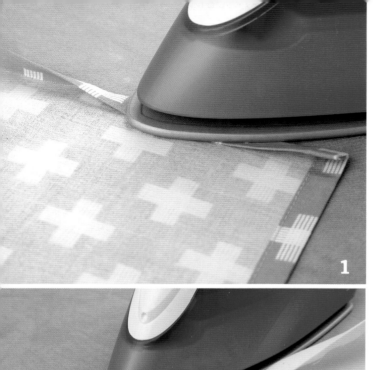

Making the half apron

1. **Assemble the apron.** With right sides facing, pin and stitch the upper apron to the lower apron along one long edge, using a ⅝" (1.5cm) seam allowance. Finish the seam allowances together with a zigzag stitch or pinking shears. Press the seam toward the lower apron. Press under ⅜" (1cm) twice on the long lower edge of the apron. Stitch close to the inner pressed edge. Repeat on the side edges.

2. **Stitch the top.** Press under ⅜" (1cm), then 1¼" (3cm) on the long upper edge of the apron. Stitch close to both pressed edges.

3. **Prepare the pocket.** Press under ⅜" (1cm), then ¾" (2cm) on the long upper edge of the pocket to form a hem. Stitch close to the lower pressed edge of the hem. Press under ⅜" (1cm) on the long lower edge and short side edges of the pocket.

4. **Attach the pocket.** With right sides facing up, pin the pocket to the center of the apron with the upper hemmed edge ¾" (2cm) above the seam. Stitch close to the side and lower edges of the pocket, stitching back and forth at the start and finish to reinforce the stitching. Stitch again ¼" (6mm) in from the pressed edges, reinforcing the stitching at the start and finish as before.

5. **Add the eyelets and ties.** Follow the manufacturer's instructions to affix a metal eyelet to the top corners of the apron, with the center of the eyelet ⅝" (1.5cm) below the upper edge and 1" (2.5cm) in from the side edges. Cut the tape in half. Press under ⅜" (1cm) on one end of each of the pieces of tape. Slip

4

each pressed end through the eyelet on the right side of the apron. Fold the pressed end up 2" (5cm) and pin to the tape. Stitch close to the pressed edge, then ¼" (6mm) in from the pressed edge. Trim the extending ends of the tapes diagonally.

5

Pear Doorstop

Choose a pretty green polka dot fabric to make this fruit-shaped doorstop. It's weighted with rice to hold a door open, and the stalk is a handle so you can move it easily. But don't get it wet!

Materials

- 20" x 12" (50 x 30m) rectangle of medium-weight sew-in interfacing
- 20" x 12" (50 x 30cm) rectangle of green polka dot cotton fabric
- 8" x 8" (20 x 20cm) square of plain brown cotton fabric
- 4" x 4" (10 x 10cm) square of plain green cotton fabric
- 3" x 2" (7.5 x 5cm) rectangle of fusible (bonding) web
- Piece of scrap paper
- Spoon
- 1½ lb. (650g) of rice
- Handful of stuffing

Cutting Out

- Find the doorstop templates on page 96.
- Cut six pears on the fold from interfacing and green polka dot fabric.
- Cut one 5" x 1¼" (13 x 3cm) bias strip for the stalk from plain brown fabric.

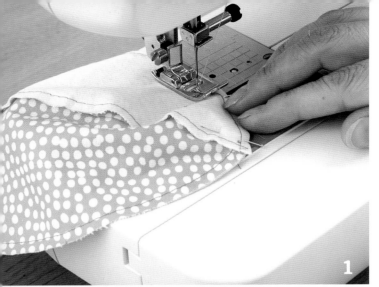

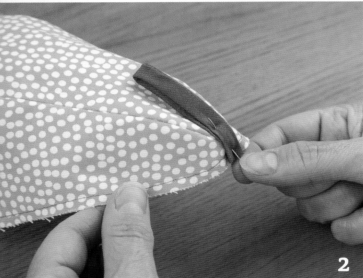

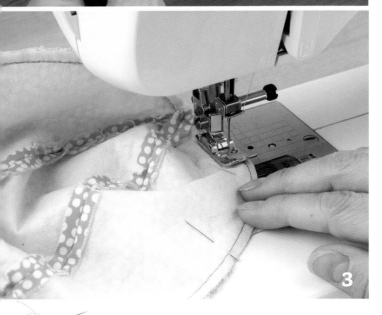

Making the doorstop

Use a ¼" (6mm) seam allowance throughout.

1. **Prepare the pear.** Baste (tack) the interfacing to the wrong side of the fabric pears. With right sides facing, pin and stitch two pears together along one edge between the dots, matching notches. Snip the curves. Press the seam open. Stitch another pear to one long edge of the first pair between the dots, right sides together and matching notches. Press the seam open. Repeat to join the other three pears.

2. **Add the stalk.** Refer to the rouleaux technique (page 15) to make the stalk. Fold the stalk in half, and pin and baste (tack) the ends to one set of pears at the dot at the narrow end.

3. **Assemble the pear.** Pin and stitch the pears together with right sides facing, matching the seams, dots, and notches and leaving a 3¼" (8cm) gap in one side edge. Stitch the stalk again just inside the first stitching to secure. Snip the curves and finger press the seam open. To finger press, open out the seam and run a moistened finger along the seam. Allow to dry before handling. Turn the pear right side out.

4. **Fill.** Roll a piece of scrap paper into a funnel and insert the narrow end into the gap. Use a spoon to tip in the rice. Fill the top of the cavity with stuffing. Slipstitch the gap closed, keeping the stitches small so the rice cannot escape.

5. **Start the leaf.** Cut the green plain fabric in half. Press fusible (bonding) web to the wrong side of one of the resulting rectangles. Peel off the backing paper and press the other rectangle, right side up, on top.

6. **Finish the leaf.** Cut out the leaf template and draw around it on the right side of the rectangle. Cut out the leaf. Press the leaf lengthwise in half, then open out again. Sew the leaf to the pear at the base of the stalk.

- -

Tip

Fill the pear three-quarters full with polystyrene micro beads instead of rice to make a fun beanbag toy for a child to play with.

- -

Quilted Oven Mitt

This colorful oven mitt is padded with layers of cotton batting (wadding) and insulated lining, all secured with rows of quilting. The mitt is long enough to protect your wrists and has a handy loop for hanging. Bear in mind, though, that the mitt is heat resistant, not heat proof.

Materials (for one mitt)

- 20" x 4" (50 x 10cm) rectangle of printed cotton fabric (fabric A)
- 20" x 12" (50 x 30cm) rectangle of printed cotton fabric (fabric B)
- 20" x 16" (50 x 40cm) rectangle of cotton batting (wadding)
- 24" x 24" (60 x 60cm) square of plain cotton fabric
- 20" x 16" (50 x 40cm) rectangle of insulated lining

Cutting Out

- Find the oven mitt template on page 103.
- Cut one 20" x 16" (50 x 40cm) rectangle for the mitt, one 6" x 1¾" (15 x 4.5cm) bias strip for the hanging loop, and one 13⅜" x 3" (34 x 7.5cm) straight strip for the binding from plain fabric.

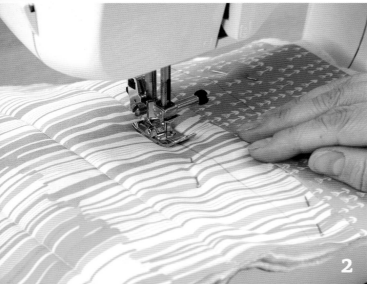

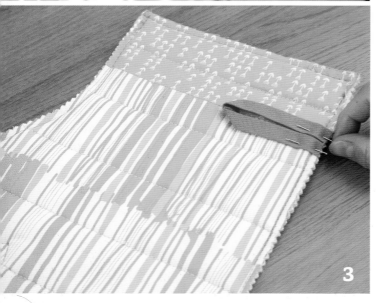

Making the mitt

Use a ⅜" (1cm) seam allowance throughout.

1. **Layer the pieces.** With right sides facing, stitch the fabric A rectangle to the fabric B rectangle along one long edge. Press the seam open. On the right side of the printed rectangle, use a sharp #2 (HB) pencil and a ruler to draw a line 1" (2.5cm) on either side of the seam. Draw four more parallel lines 2" (5cm) apart on fabric B. Place the cotton batting (wadding) on the wrong side of the plain fabric rectangle. Add the insulated lining, shiny side up if it has one, then the printed rectangle, right side up, on top.

2. **Quilt the mitt.** Smooth the fabrics out from the center, then pin the layers together. Starting on the center line, stitch along the drawn lines, smoothing the fabric outward as you stitch to quilt the rectangle. Use the template to cut out a pair of mitts, one at a time, from the quilted fabric. Use a pair of pinking shears to cut the curved edges; match the dotted lines to the quilting, and the solid line to the seam. Baste (tack) the outer edges.

3. **Make the hanging loop.** Refer to the rouleaux technique (page 15) to make the hanging loop. Press the loop flat. Pin and baste (tack) the ends of the loop to the right side of one mitt on either side of the cross.

4. **Combine the halves.** Pin the mitts together with the printed sides facing and matching the seams. Stitch the outer edges, leaving the straight edges open. Stitch again for 1¼" (3cm) on either side of the "V" at the dot, just inside the first stitching, to reinforce the seam. Carefully snip the seam allowance almost to the dot.

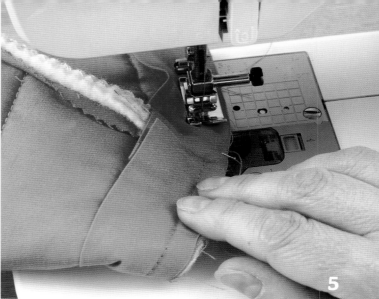

5. **Add the binding.** Press the binding lengthwise in half with wrong sides facing, then press under ¼" (6mm) at one end. Starting at the pressed-under end, pin the binding to the lower edge of the plain side of the mitt, matching the raw edges and overlapping the ends of the binding. Stitch the binding to the mitt. The process will be easier if you can remove the bed of the sewing machine and slip the mitt over the arm of the machine.

6. **Finish the binding.** Turn the mitt right side out. Turn the binding over the raw edge so that it just covers the seam. Pin and baste (tack) in place. Topstitch close to the pressed edge of the binding.

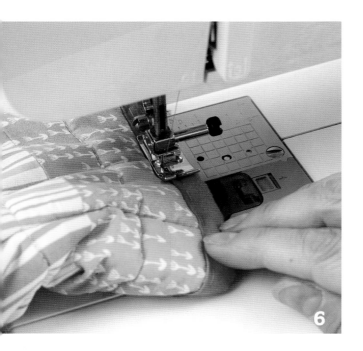

Tip

If you don't have a pair of pinking shears, finish the curved raw edges of the mitts with a zigzag stitch after cutting them out.

Stacked Pincushion

A small, square cushion is the simplest way to make a pincushion, but a stack of squares fastened with a pretty ribbon and button looks far more impressive!

Materials

- 10" x 6" (25 x 15cm) rectangles of three printed cotton fabrics
- 2 oz. (60g) wood shavings or sawdust
- 24" (60cm) of ⅝" (1.5cm)-wide printed ribbon
- One ¾" (2cm) flat button
- Piece of scrap paper
- Two or four pearl- or glass-headed dressmaking pins

Cutting Out

- Cut two 4⅜" (11cm) squares from each of the three fabrics.

Tip

Use this method to make a stack of fragrant potpourri sachets by filling the squares with dried lavender and sewing the button on top rather than pinning it.

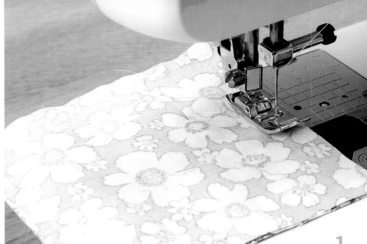

Making the pincushion

1. **Make the cushions.** With right sides facing and using a ¼" (6mm) seam allowance, pin and stitch each pair of squares together around the outer edges, leaving a 2⅜" (6cm) gap in the center of one edge. Clip the corners, then turn the squares right side out. Fold under the seam allowance along the edges of the gap.

2. **Fill the cushions.** Roll a piece of scrap paper into a funnel and insert the narrow end into one square. Tip in wood shavings or sawdust to firmly fill the cavity. Slipstitch the gap closed, keeping the stitches small so the filling cannot escape. Repeat to fill the other squares, then stack the filled squares one on top of the other.

3. **Assemble the pincushion.** Cut the ribbon in half. Wrap one ribbon tightly around the squares, overlapping the ends at the center by about ⅝" (1.5cm). Cut off the excess ribbon and sew the overlapped ends together. Pin one end of the remaining ribbon at a right angle across the ends of the first ribbon. Wrap the ribbon tightly around the squares, overlapping the ends by about ⅝" (1.5cm). Cut off the excess ribbon and sew securely to the top square. Position a button on top of the intersection and secure with a dressmaking pin through each hole of the button.

Headphones Case

Keep your headphones safe (and maybe even untangled!) in this cute case. The zippered fastening makes the contents easily accessible, and the attached key ring allows you to secure the case to a belt loop or bag handle. Of course, the case is ideal for storing all sorts of other small items, too—use it as a coin purse or for whatever little items you want to carry.

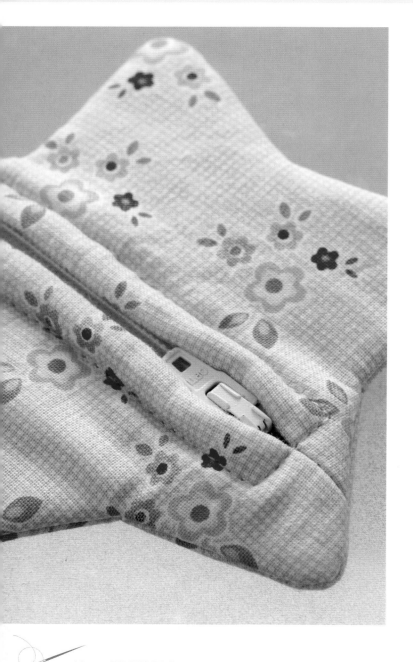

Materials

- 12" x 8" (30 x 20cm) rectangle of printed cotton fabric
- 12" x 8" (30 x 20cm) rectangle of lightweight white cotton fabric
- 12" x 8" (30 x 20cm) rectangle of lightweight batting (wadding)
- 12" x 8" (30 x 20cm) rectangle of plain cotton fabric
- One 4" (10cm) zipper
- One ¾" (2cm) diameter key ring

Cutting Out

- Find the headphones case templates on page 101.
- Cut one upper front on the fold, one lower front on the fold, and one back on the fold from printed fabric, lightweight white fabric, batting (wadding), and plain fabric.
- Cut one 2" x 1½" (5 x 4cm) rectangle on the bias (see page 13) for the hanging loop from printed fabric.

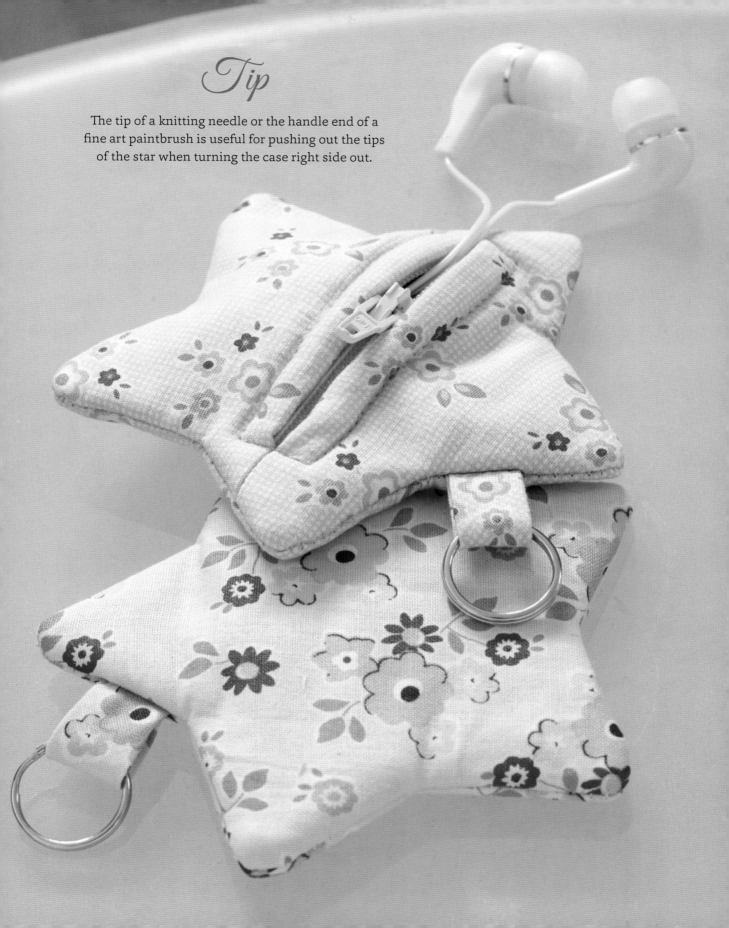

Tip

The tip of a knitting needle or the handle end of a
fine art paintbrush is useful for pushing out the tips
of the star when turning the case right side out.

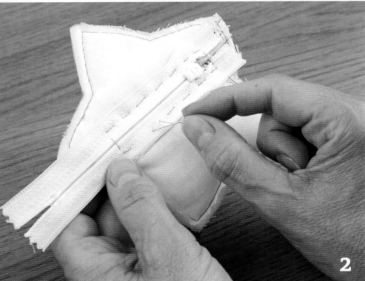

Making the headphones case

1. **Start the front.** Place the upper front and lower front batting (wadding) pieces on the white lightweight fabric pieces, then place the printed upper front and lower front right side up on top. Pin and baste (tack) the layers together. Pin the upper and lower printed fronts together with right sides facing, matching the long, straight edge. Using a ½" (1.2cm) seam allowance, stitch the long, straight edge, leaving a gap between the dots. Baste (tack) along the gap. Press the seam open.

2. **Add the zipper.** On the wrong side, mark the position of the dots with pins across the seam. Place the zipper face down on the wrong side centrally along the basted (tacked) seam with the slider ¼" (6mm) below one pin. Pin and baste (tack) the zipper to the front, basting (tacking) across the zipper at the pinned marks.

3. **Stitch the zipper.** On the right side, use a zipper foot to stitch the zipper ⁵⁄₁₆" (8mm) on either side of the seam and across the zipper just outside the basting (tacking) across the zipper. Cut off the ends of the zipper ⁵⁄₃₂" (4mm) beyond the stitching across the zipper.

4. **Make the front lining.** Use a ½" (1.2cm) seam allowance to stitch the plain fabric upper and lower fronts together along the long edges, leaving a gap between the dots. Press the seam open. Pin the front lining to the front star with right sides facing out, matching the seam. Baste (tack) the outer edges. Pin and slipstitch the pressed edges of the lining around the zipper.

5. **Make the back.** Pin the back batting (wadding) on the wrong side of the plain back. Pin the printed back right side up

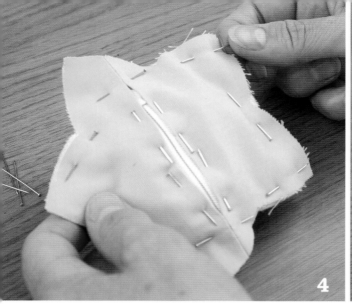

on top. Baste (tack) the outer edges. Refer to the rouleaux technique (page 15) to make the hanging loop. Press the loop flat. Slip the loop through a key ring and pin the raw ends together. Pin and baste (tack) the raw ends to the right side of the back 1" (2.5cm) from one tip.

6. **Assemble the star.** Open the zipper. Pin the stars together with the printed sides facing. Stitch the outer edges, using a ¼" (6mm) seam allowance.

7. **Finish the case.** Carefully press the seam allowance to flatten the batting (wadding). Clip the corners, but not too close to the stitching at the tips, because you need to leave room to finish (neaten) the seam. Finish the seam allowances closed with a zigzag stitch or with a pair of pinking shears. Carefully snip to the inner corners. Turn the case right side out.

Key Case

We all know someone who constantly misplaces their keys. Make this compact key case and their precious keys will never go astray again. The key rings inside the flexible case allow the keys to be used while still attached to the case. The case folds flat, but opens to form a box, so it's ideal for storing other small items, too.

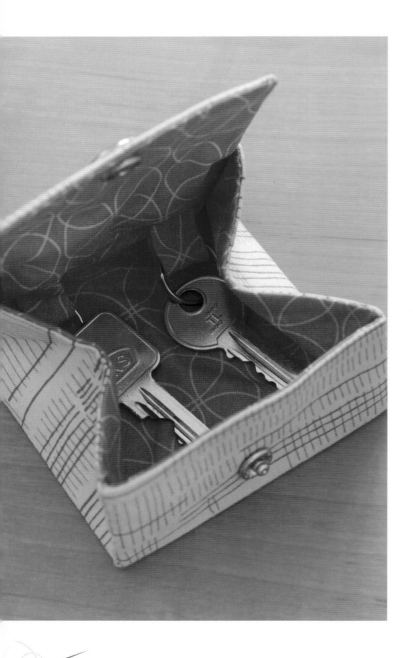

Materials

- 14" x 8" (35 x 20cm) rectangle of printed cotton fabric (fabric A) for the lining
- 12" x 10" (30 x 25cm) rectangle of printed cotton fabric (fabric B) for the outer case
- 12" x 10" (30 x 25cm) rectangle of firm iron-on interfacing
- Two ¾" (2cm) diameter key rings
- One ⅝" (1.5cm) snap closure and setting tool

Cutting Out

- Find the key case template on page 98.
- Cut one key case on the fold from fabric A, cutting along the lining cutting line. Also cut two 2" x 1½" (5 x 4cm) rectangles on the bias for hanging loops and one 4" x 3¼" (10 x 8cm) rectangle for the flap lining from fabric A.
- Cut one key case on the fold from fabric B and interfacing, cutting along the outer case cutting line.

Making the key case

Use a ¼" (6mm) seam allowance throughout and stitch seams with right sides facing.

1. **Make the key ring pieces.** Refer to the rouleaux technique (page 15) to make the hanging loops. Press the loops flat. Slip each loop through a key ring and pin the raw ends together. Pin and stitch the loops to one long edge on the right side of the flap lining ¾" (2cm) in from the short edges, matching the raw edges.

2. **Assemble the lining.** Stitch the edge of the flap lining that has the loops to the flap edge of the lining case, leaving a 2½" (6.5cm) gap in the center to turn through later. Press the seam open.

3. **Combine the outside and lining.** Press the interfacing to the wrong side of the fabric B case. Pin the cases together with right sides facing. Stitch the outer edges. Clip the outer corners and carefully snip to the inner corners.

4. **Add the fastener.** Turn the case right side out. Slipstitch the gap closed. Press the case. With the lining inside, refer to the template to press the case along one dotted line. Open out the case and repeat on each dotted line. Follow the manufacturer's instructions to fix a snap closure at the dots on the right side of the case with the top (female) section on the flap and lower (male) section on the front.

5. **Create the box shape.** Bring two adjacent short edges together. Use a double length of sewing thread to slipstitch the edges together with small, neat stitches, pushing the lining inside as you stitch. Stitch back and forth at the top to reinforce. Repeat at each corner to form a box.

6. **Fold the case.** Push in the side edges, then fold the front on top. Slip your finger under the front and crease with a fingernail along the diagonal folds that have formed on the side edges. Fold the flap on top.

Tip

For a precision finish, make sure that you cut the cases and stitch the outer edges carefully and accurately.

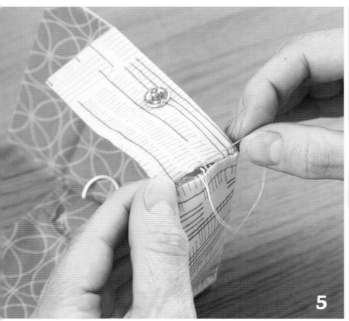

Kimono Clothespin Bag

Bring a well-deserved touch of glamour to laundry days with a kimono-style clothespin bag. There is a generous pocket for storing clothespins and a hook at the top to hang the kimono on the clothesline.

Materials

- 16" (40cm) of 44" (112cm)-wide printed cotton fabric (fabric A)
- 30" (75cm) of 36" (90cm)-wide medium-weight sew-in interfacing
- 16" (40cm) square of printed cotton fabric (fabric B)
- Child's clothes hanger
- Frog fastening

Cutting Out

- Find the clothespin bag template on page 102.
- Cut one pair of fronts and one back on the fold from fabric A and interfacing.
- Cut one 15" x 3¼" (38 x 8cm) rectangle for the collar and one 11" x 9⅞" (28 x 25cm) rectangle for the pocket from fabric B.

Tip

If you don't have a frog fastening, sew on
a pair of buttons, one on either side of the
front edge just below the collar.

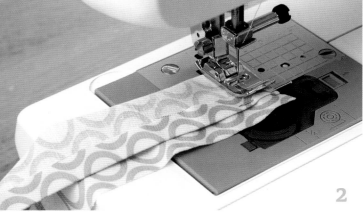

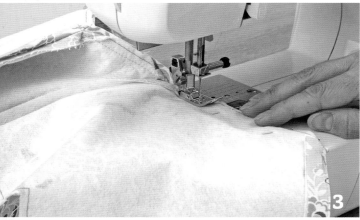

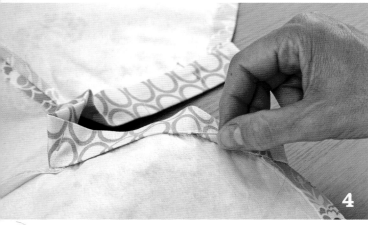

Making the clothespin bag

Use a ⅜" (1cm) seam allowance throughout.

1. **Start the kimono.** Pin and baste (tack) interfacing to the wrong side of the fronts and back. Press under ⅝" (1.5cm) on the long edges of the front and stitch in place close to the pressed edges. Stitch the fronts to the back along the shoulder seams between the dots. Press the seams open.

2. **Start the collar.** Press the collar lengthwise in half with wrong sides facing, then open out and press under ⅜" (1cm) on one long edge. Fold the ends of the collar along the center fold line with the right sides facing. Stitch the ends. Clip the corners then turn right side out.

3. **Add the collar.** With right sides facing, pin and stitch the neck edge of the fronts and back to the long raw edge of the collar. Refer to the grading (layering) seam allowances technique (page 12) to grade the seam allowances.

4. **Finish the collar.** Press the seam toward the collar. Pin the pressed edge of the collar along the neck seam. Slipstitch the pressed edge to the neck seam.

5. **Cross the kimono front.** With right sides facing up, overlap the right-hand front over the left-hand front, matching the centers. Pin in place, then topstitch 5⁄16" (8mm) in from the right-hand front edge. Catch the front neck seams together where they overlap with a few discreet stitches.

6. **Add the pocket.** With wrong sides facing, fold the pocket in half parallel with the short edges. Press the folded edge. Pin and baste (tack) the pocket to the right side of the front, matching the raw edges.

7. **Sew up the kimono.** Fold the clothespin bag along the shoulder seams with right sides facing, matching the raw edges. Pin and stitch the raw edges, starting and finishing at the dots and leaving a 5½" (14cm) gap in the center of the lower edge. Clip the outer corners, then carefully snip to the inner corners. Turn the clothespin bag right side out. Press the lower edge and press under the edges of the gap.

8. **Finish the bag.** Insert the clothes hanger into the clothespin bag and slip the hook through the neck opening. Pin the gap on the lower edge closed. Topstitch ³⁄₁₆" (5mm) above the lower edge. For decoration, sew the frog fastening across the front edge just below the collar.

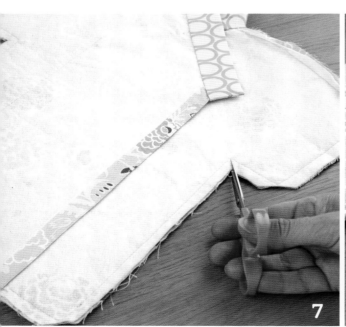

Laptop Case

Cases for laptops usually have a bland, hi-tech style. But it doesn't have to be that way. Choose the prettiest floral and daintiest polka dot fabrics to make a case full of Old World charm. This zippered version is softly padded and has a removable shoulder strap to leave your hands free when you are out and about.

Materials

- 6" (15cm) of 44" (112cm)-wide polka dot cotton fabric
- 16" (40cm) of 44" (112cm)-wide printed cotton fabric
- 14" (35cm) of 36" (90cm)-wide lightweight batting (wadding)
- 16" (40cm) of 36" (90cm)-wide medium-weight sew-in interfacing
- 30" x 16" (75 x 40cm) rectangle of plain cotton fabric
- 30" (75cm) zipper
- Two 1¼" (3cm) metal rings
- Two swivel bolt snaps

Cutting Out

- Cut two 12⅜" x 4⅛" (31.5 x 10.5cm) rectangles for the bands, two 2¼" x 2¼" (6 x 6cm) squares for the ring holders, and two 2" x 1" (5 x 2.5cm) rectangles for the zipper end covers from polka dot fabric.
- Cut two 12⅜" x 12⅜" (31.5 x 31.5cm) squares for the case and one 36" x 2¾" (90 x 7cm) strip for the strap from printed fabric.
- Cut two 15¾" x 12⅜" (40 x 31.5cm) rectangles of lightweight batting (wadding), interfacing, and plain fabric for the lining.
- Cut two 2¼" x 2¼" (6 x 6 cm) squares for the ring holders and one 36" x 2" (90 x 5cm) strip for the strap from interfacing.

Tip

A standard 13" x 9" (33 x 23cm) laptop
fits this case. Make the case wider and
longer for a larger laptop.

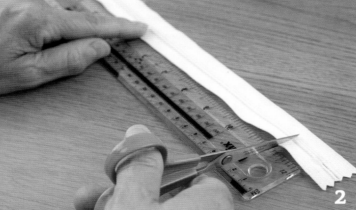

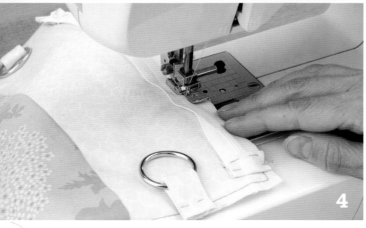

Making the laptop case

Use a ⅜" (1cm) seam allowance throughout.

1. **Start the case.** With right sides facing, stitch one long edge of each band to the upper edge of each case. Press the seams toward the cases. Place the batting (wadding) on the interfacing cases, then pin the fabric cases right side up on top. Baste (tack) the outer edges. Pin and baste (tack) interfacing to the wrong side of the ring holders. Fold the holders in half with right sides facing. Stitch the long edge. Refer to the grading (layering) seam allowances technique (page 12) to grade the seam allowances. Refer to step 2 of the rouleaux technique (page 15) to turn through. Slip each holder through a metal ring and pin the raw edges together. Pin and baste (tack) the holders to the short side edges of one band 1⅜" (4.5cm) below the upper edge.

2. **Prepare the zipper.** Close the zipper. Cut across the tape ⅜" (1cm) above the slider. Cut across the zipper 11¼" (28.5cm) from the cut end.

3. **Add the zipper covers.** Press under ⅜" (1cm) on the short edges of the zipper end covers. With wrong sides facing, press the covers in half parallel with the pressed edges. Slightly open the zipper. Slip each end of the zipper into a zipper end cover with the raw edges of the covers level with the long edges of the zipper. Baste (tack) in place through all the layers.

4. **Add the zipper.** With the zipper centered and right sides facing, pin one long edge of the zipper to the upper edge of one band. Use a zipper foot to stitch in place. Repeat to stitch the other long edge of the zipper to the other

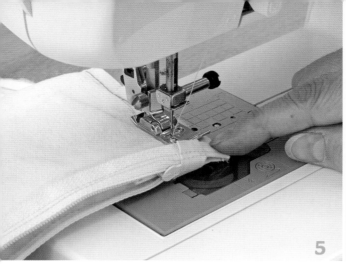

5

6

band. Press the bands away from the zipper. Topstitch close to the zipper teeth.

5. **Continue the case.** Open the zipper. Pin the case and bands together with right sides facing and matching the seams. Stitch the raw edges. Clip the corners. Press the seam open by running the tip of the iron along the seam to avoid flattening the batting (wadding).

6. **Add the lining.** Press under ⅜" (1cm) on the short upper edges of the linings. With right sides facing, pin and stitch the linings together along the raw edges. Clip the corners and press the seams open. Turn the lining right side out. Insert the case into the lining, matching the seams. Pin and slipstitch the pressed edges of the lining

around the zipper and upper corners of the case. Turn the case right side out.

7. **Make the strap.** Lay the interfacing strap along the center on the wrong side of the fabric strap. Press the long edges of the fabric over the interfacing. Press the strap lengthwise in half with wrong sides facing. Topstitch close to the long pressed edges, stitching both edges in the same direction to avoid dragging the fabric.

8. **Attach the strap.** Press under ⅜" (1cm) on the ends of the strap. Slip each end through the loop of a swivel bolt snap. Fold up the pressed end for 1½" (4cm) and pin to the strap. Stitch close to the pressed edge, then ¼" (6mm) below the pressed edge. Clip the bolt snaps onto the rings.

7

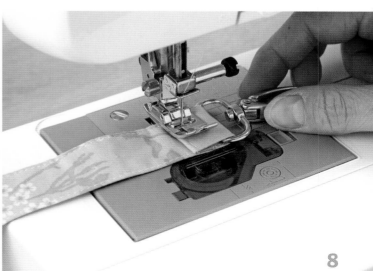

8

Leaf Place Mat

It is very easy to make a set of flamboyant leaf-shaped place mats. The mats are heat resistant, as they are padded with cotton batting (wadding) and insulated lining. Using a different printed fabric for each side of the mats makes them reversible, and they have a handy loop for hanging elsewhere when not in use.

Materials (for one mat)

- 14" x 12" (35 x 30cm) rectangle of printed cotton fabric (fabric A)
- 14" x 12" (35 x 30cm) rectangle of printed cotton fabric (fabric B)
- 14" x 12" (35 x 30cm) rectangle of cotton batting (wadding)
- 14" x 12" (35 x 30cm) rectangle of insulated lining
- Cotton sewing thread in contrasting color
- 48" (1.2m) of ¾" (2cm)-wide bias binding
- One ⅝" (1.5cm) button

Cutting Out

- Find the place mat template on page 99.
- Cut one leaf from fabric A, fabric B, cotton batting (wadding), and insulated lining.

Making the place mat

1. **Assemble the leaf.** Refer to the template to draw the leaf veins with a sharp #2 (HB) pencil and ruler on the right side of the fabric A leaf. With the outer edges level, place the cotton batting (wadding) leaf on the wrong side of the fabric B leaf, then the insulated lining on top, with the shiny side facing up if it has one. Place the fabric A leaf on top of that. Smooth the layers out from the center and pin together. Baste (tack) the outer edges. Using cotton sewing thread of a contrasting color, stitch along the drawn lines to quilt the leaf.

2. **Attach the binding.** Open out one edge of the binding. Starting at the tip of the leaf, pin the binding to the underside of the leaf, matching the raw edges. Stitch along the fold line of the binding to about 2" (5cm) from the tip of the leaf.

3. **Continue the binding.** Fold the binding at the start of the stitching to the front of the leaf and pin the pressed edge just over the seam on the front. Turn the leaf over and continue stitching along the fold line.

4. **Finish the binding.** Cut off the excess binding ½" (1.2cm) beyond the tip of the leaf. Lay the end of the binding away from the leaf and fold and pin the end neatly over the tip of the leaf. Fold the binding to the front of the leaf and pin the pressed edge just over the seam. Hand sew the binding in place at the tip. Stitch close to the pressed edge of the entire binding.

5. **Add the loop.** Cut a 10" (25cm) length of the remaining binding for the hanging loop. Press the binding open, then fold it lengthwise in half with right sides facing. Pin and stitch along the fold line.

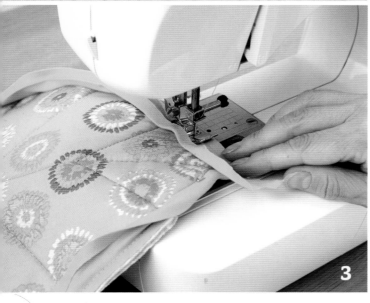

4

Trim the seam allowance to ³⁄₁₆" (4mm). Refer to step 2 of the rouleaux technique (page 15) to turn the loop right side out with a bodkin. Press the loop flat. Poke in the ends and slipstitch them closed. Overlap the ends of the loop by 1¼" (3cm) and pin to the top of the leaf. Sew in place, then sew a button onto the overlap.

Tip

Enlarge or reduce the template to change the size of the mats—they would make a practical set in different sizes and look very sweet as coasters, too.

5

Buttoned Mug Hug

Keep your favorite beverage hot with a pretty embroidered mug hug. The dimensions are ideal for a standard 3¾" (9.5cm)-tall mug, but they can be changed to suit your own dishware by making the hug longer, shorter, taller, or narrower, as you need.

Materials

- 12" x 4" (30 x 10cm) rectangles of two coordinating printed cotton fabrics
- 12" x 4" (30 x 10cm) rectangle of lightweight batting (wadding)
- 12" x 4" (30 x 10cm) rectangle of lightweight white cotton fabric
- 16" x 16" (40 x 40cm) square of plain cotton fabric
- Embroidery floss to match plain fabric
- ½" (1.2cm) bias binding maker
- One ⅝" (1.5cm) button

Cutting Out

- Cut one 11⅜" x 1⅝" (29 x 4cm) strip of one printed fabric and one 11⅜" x 2⅛" (29 x 5.5cm) strip of the other printed fabric for the outer hug.
- Cut one 11⅜" x 3" (29 x 7.5cm) rectangle of lightweight white fabric, batting (wadding), and plain fabric.
- Cut one 2½" x 1" (7 x 2.5cm) bias strip for the button loop and two 11⅜" x 1" (29 x 2.5cm) bias strips for the binding from plain fabric.

Making the mug hug

1. **Make the outer hug.** With right sides facing and using a ⅜" (1cm) seam allowance, pin and stitch the printed rectangles together along one long edge to make the outer hug. Press the seam open. Use an air-erasable pen to draw a loopy squiggly line over the seam on the right side of the outer hug, starting and finishing ⅝" (1.5cm) in from the short edges. Separate and use three strands of embroidery floss threaded onto a crewel needle to embroider the drawn line with a chain stitch. To embroider a chain stitch, knot the ends to start and bring the needle to the right side at one end of the line. Insert the needle back through the same hole and bring the needle out about ³⁄₁₆" (5mm) along the line, keeping the thread under the needle. Pull the thread through and continue along the line. Finish with a knot in the wrong side.

2. **Layer the pieces.** Place the batting (wadding) rectangle on the lightweight fabric rectangle, then place the embroidered hug, right side up, on top. Smooth the fabrics out from the center and pin the layers together. Baste (tack) around the outer edges.

3. **Make the loop.** Refer to the rouleaux technique (page 15) to make the button loop. Pin and baste (tack) the ends of the loop to the center of one short edge on the right side of the outer hug.

4. **Attach the back.** Pin the outer hug to the plain rectangle with right sides facing. Stitch the short edges, using a ⅜" (1cm) seam allowance. Carefully trim away the batting (wadding) in the seam allowances. Turn the hug right side out and press the short edges. Pin and baste (tack) the raw edges together.

5. **Start the binding.** Refer to the bias binding technique (page 14) to make

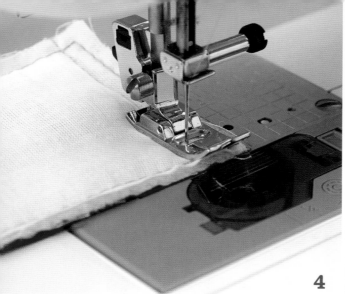

4

5

two ½" (1.2cm)-wide bindings. See step 1 of the single-fold binding technique (page 14) to stitch one binding to one long edge on the right side, with the binding extending equally beyond the short edges. Repeat to stitch the other binding to the other long edge.

6. **Finish the binding.** Lightly press the bindings away from the hug. Fold and pin the ends of the bindings over the ends of the seams. See step 2 of the single-fold binding technique (page 14) to finish the bindings. Wrap the hug around your chosen mug and mark the button position with a pin under the button loop. Remove the hug and sew the button in place.

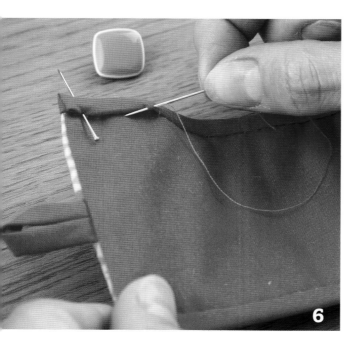

6

Tip

If you prefer to use ready-made binding, press open a 2½" (7cm) length of bias binding to make a matching button loop.

Needle Case

This pretty birdhouse-shaped needle case is sturdy enough to stand up, so it makes a charming and practical decoration for the sewing room. The front cover has a bird-shaped button perched on an embroidered branch and opens to reveal felt pages to store your sewing needles.

Materials

- 12" x 10" (30 x 25cm) rectangle of iron-on firm interfacing
- 10" x 6" (25 x 15cm) rectangle of polka dot cotton fabric
- 12" x 10" (30 x 25cm) rectangle of printed cotton fabric
- Masking tape
- 9" (23cm) square of felt
- Dark gray embroidery floss
- One bird-shaped button

Cutting Out

- Find the needle case templates on page 94.
- Cut two pairs of covers from iron-on firm interfacing.
- Cut one pair of covers each from polka dot and printed fabric.
- Cut four roofs from printed fabric.
- Cut four pages from felt.

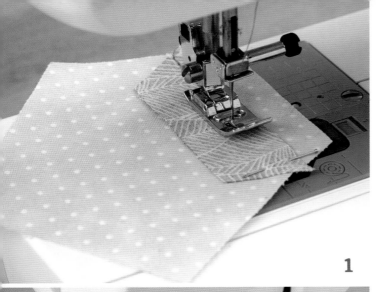

Making the needle case

1. **Start the roofs.** Press the interfacing covers to the wrong side of the fabric covers. With right sides facing, pin one roof to one polka dot cover with the long edge ⅝" (1.5cm) in from the right-hand slanted edge. Stitch the long roof edge, using a ¼" (6mm) seam allowance on the roof. Press the roof upwards, matching the raw edges.

2. **Add the other roofs.** Stitch a roof to the left-hand slanted edge in the same way. Repeat to stitch roofs to the other polka dot cover.

3. **Draw the details.** Trace the cover template onto tracing paper with a sharp #2 (HB) pencil, adding the circle and branch. Turn the tracing over and redraw the circle and branch with the pencil. Use masking tape to tape the tracing right side up on the right side of one polka dot cover. Redraw the circle and branch to transfer them to the fabric.

4. **Embroider.** Separate and use four strands of embroidery floss to embroider the circle and branch with a backstitch. To embroider a backstitch, bring the needle out on the circle, make a backward stitch ⁵⁄₃₂" (4mm) long, and bring the needle one stitch length ahead. Continue along the line. Embroider the branch in the same way, starting ⁵⁄₃₂" (4mm) from one end of the line.

5. **Finish the covers.** Pin and stitch the polka dot covers to the printed covers with right sides facing, using a ¼" (6mm) seam allowance and leaving a 2¼" (5.5cm) gap in the lower edge to turn through. Refer to the grading (layering) seam allowances technique (page 12) to grade the seam allowances, then clip the corners. Turn right side out and press. Slipstitch the gap closed.

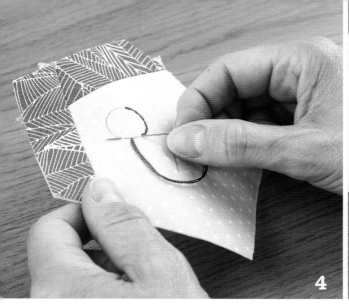

6. **Layer the case.** With the left-hand edges level, place the pages on the printed side of the unembroidered cover with the embroidered cover, right side up, on top.

7. **Finish the case.** Baste (tack) the left-hand edge through all the layers. Stitch ¼" (6mm) in from the left-hand edge. Sew a bird shaped button to the cover "perched" on the embroidered branch.

Tip

When basting (tacking) the pages between the covers, insert the needle at right angles to the covers to keep the left-hand edges level and to avoid dislodging the layers.

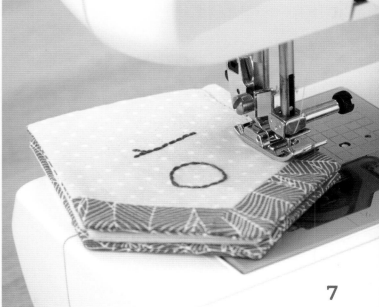

Pot Holder

Cute enough to display in the kitchen, this sky-themed pot holder has sun- and cloud-shaped pockets to slip your hand into for protection when carrying hot pots and plates. Bear in mind that the pot holder is heat resistant, not heat proof.

Materials

- 14" x 8" (35 x 20cm) rectangle of yellow cotton fabric
- 10" x 8" (25 x 20cm) rectangle of white cotton fabric
- 16" x 12" (40 x 30cm) rectangle of cotton batting (wadding)
- 16" x 10" (40 x 25cm) rectangle of light blue printed cotton fabric
- 10" x 8" (25 x 20cm) rectangle of insulated lining
- Light blue embroidery floss
- 1 yd. (90cm) of ¾" (2cm)-wide light blue bias binding
- One ⅝" (1.5cm) yellow button

Cutting Out

- Find the pot holder templates on page 97.
- Cut five pairs of sunbeams and two suns on the fold from yellow fabric.
- Cut two clouds on the fold from white fabric.
- Cut one sun on the fold, one cloud on the fold, five sunbeams, and one oval on the fold from cotton batting (wadding).
- Cut two ovals on the fold from light blue printed fabric.
- Cut one oval on the fold from insulated lining.

Tip

A pretty fabric printed with clouds has been used here for the oval; a light blue polka dot fabric would achieve a similar sky effect.

Making the pot holder

1. **Make the sunbeams.** Place the yellow sunbeams together in five pairs with right sides facing. Pin the batting (wadding) sunbeams on top. Stitch the straight edges, using a ¼" (6mm) seam allowance. Carefully trim away the batting (wadding) in the seam allowance. Clip the corners. Turn right side out and press.

2. **Attach the sunbeams.** Baste (tack) one sun right side up on the batting (wadding) sun. Pin and baste (tack) the sunbeams on top with right sides facing, matching the dots and raw edges.

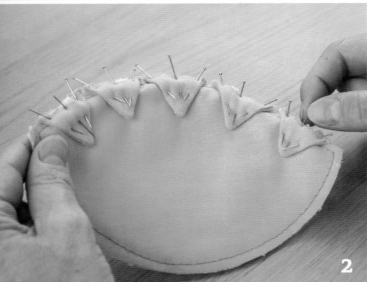

3. **Start the cloud.** Use a sharp #2 (HB) pencil to trace the raindrops onto the right side of one white cloud. Separate and use three strands of light blue embroidery floss to embroider the raindrops with a satin stitch. To embroider a satin stitch, work straight, parallel stitches side by side diagonally across the teardrop, without any gaps between stitches. Press the embroidery face down on a towel to avoid flattening the stitches. Baste (tack) the embroidered cloud right side up on the batting (wadding) cloud.

4. **Assemble the cloud and sun.** Pin the suns together and clouds together with right sides facing. Stitch the unnotched edges, using a ¼" (6mm) seam allowance. Carefully trim away the batting (wadding) in the seam allowances. Snip to the inner corners on the cloud. Snip the curves on the sun and the cloud. Turn right side out and press the seams. Pin the raw edges together.

5. **Put the clouds and sun in the sky.** Place the cotton batting (wadding) on the wrong side of one printed oval. Add the insulated lining, shiny side up if it has one, then the other printed oval, right side up, on top. Baste (tack) the outer edges. With right

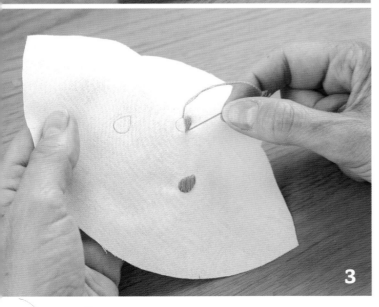

sides facing up, pin and baste (tack) the sun and cloud on top, matching the notches.

6. **Add the binding.** Open out one end of the binding and fold under ¼" (6mm). Refer to the single-fold binding technique (page 14) to pin the binding to the right side of the oval, starting at the pressed under end and cutting off the other end ⅜" (1cm) beyond the start. Overlap the ends of the binding. Follow the technique to bind the oval and slipstitch to the underside.

7. **Make the loop.** Cut one 8" (20cm) length of bias binding for the hanging loop. Lightly press open the binding. Fold the binding lengthwise in half with right sides facing. Pin and stitch along the fold line. Trim the seam allowance. Turn the loop right side out, referring to step 2 of the rouleaux technique (page 15). Turn in the ends and slipstitch them closed, then press the loop flat. Bend the loop in half and pin to the top of the oval, overlapping the ends diagonally by ¾" (2cm). Sew to the oval with a button at the overlap.

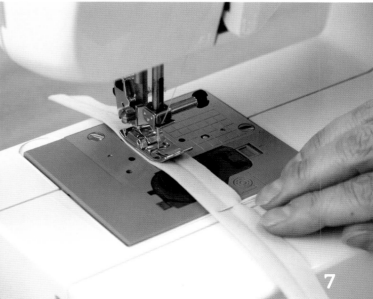

Panel Pillow

A simple pillow is often the first project attempted by a new sewer, and this charming example is easy enough for a beginner to tackle. The three printed panels on the front are secured edge-to-edge with a set of buttons to reveal glimpses of the plain fabric underneath.

Materials

- 20" x 14" (50 x 35cm) rectangle of printed cotton fabric, short edges parallel with selvages
- 28" x 14" (70 x 35cm) rectangle of plain cotton fabric
- Four ¾" (2cm) flower-shaped buttons
- 12" (30cm) pillow form (cushion pad)

Cutting Out

- Cut two 12¾" x 5⅞" (32 x 15cm) rectangles for the side panels and one 12¾" x 7" (32 x 18cm) rectangle for the center panel from printed fabric.
- Cut two 12¾" x 12¾" (32 x 32cm) squares for the front and back from plain fabric.

If you would prefer to have an envelope opening on the back of the pillow, cut two 12¾" x 9" (32 x 23cm) rectangles instead of the square, and follow steps 5–7 from the Chenille Sofa Pillow instructions on page 16.

Making the pillow

1. **Start the panels.** Press under 1½" (4cm) on the long right-hand edge of one side panel, the long left-hand edge of the other side panel, and both long edges of the center panel. On the right side, topstitch 1¼" (3cm) from the pressed edges.

2. **Finish the front.** With right sides facing up, pin the panels to the front, matching the raw edges and butting the pressed edges together. Baste (tack) the outer edges. Stitch the center of the lower edge for 10¾" (26cm), using a ⅜" (1cm) seam allowance. Catch the pressed edges together 3⅛" (8cm) inside the top and bottom raw edges. Sew a button on top at each position.

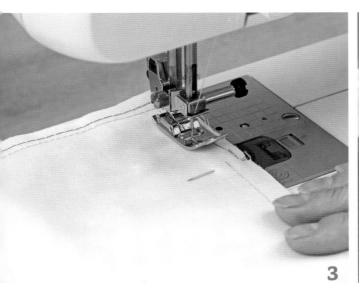

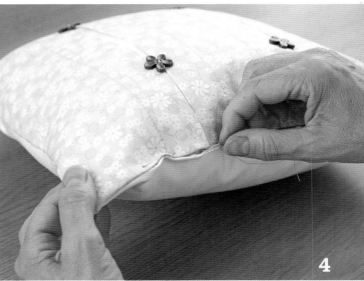

3. **Assemble the halves.** Pin the front and back together with right sides facing, matching the raw edges. Stitch the outer edges, using a ⅜" (1cm) seam allowance and starting and finishing at the ends of the stitching on the lower edge.

4. **Finish the pillow.** Clip the corners and turn the pillow cover right side out. Insert the pillow form (cushion pad). Turn under the edges of the gap and pin them together. Slipstitch the gap closed.

Hanging Storage Tub

A set of fabulous storage tubs would be a handy addition for any room in your home. Each tub is stiffened with interfacing so it will stand upright on a surface, or you can hang it on a hook with its loop. A channel at the top, threaded with plastic boning, holds the rim open.

Materials (for one tub)

- 14" x 10" (35 x 25cm) rectangle of printed cotton fabric (fabric A)
- 14" x 10" (35 x 25cm) rectangle of medium weight sew-in interfacing
- 16" x 12" (40 x 30cm) rectangle of printed cotton fabric (fabric B)
- 14" (36cm) of ⅜" (1cm)-wide plastic boning

Cutting Out

- Cut one 12⅝" x 4½" (32 x 11.5cm) rectangle for the tub and one 4½" (11.5cm) diameter circle for the base from fabric A and medium-weight sew-in interfacing.
- Cut one 7¼" x 2¼" (18 x 6cm) rectangle for the loop, one 12⅝" x 6" (32 x 15.5cm) rectangle for the tub lining, and one 4½" (11.5cm) diameter circle for the base lining from fabric B.

Tip

A sleeve ironing board is particularly useful when pressing the storage tub, as the end of the board will fit neatly inside the tub.

Making the storage tub

Use a ⅜" (1cm) seam allowance throughout.

1. **Start the outer tub.** Pin the tub and base pieces right side up on the interfacing pieces. Baste (tack) the outer edges. Fold the tub in half parallel with the short edges with right sides facing. Stitch the short edges and press the seam open. Fold the lower edge of the tub and circumference of the base into quarters and mark each division with a pin.

2. **Assemble the outer tub.** Snip the lower edge of the tub at regular intervals, making the snips about ⁵⁄₁₆" (0.75mm) deep and ⅜" (1cm) apart. This will make the seam allowance lay flat when you stitch it to the base. With right sides facing, pin and stitch the lower edge of the tub to the base, matching the divisions. Refer to the grading (layering) seam allowances technique (page 12) to trim the seam allowance. Snip the curves and press the seam toward the tub. Turn the tub right side out.

3. **Make the loop.** Fold the loop lengthwise in half with right sides facing. Stitch the long edge. Refer to step 2 of the rouleaux technique (page 15) to turn the loop right side out. Press the loop, then topstitch close to both long edges. Pin and baste (tack) the ends of the loop to the right side of the tub, on either side of the seam.

4. **Make the lining.** Fold the tub lining in half parallel with the short edges with right sides facing. Stitch the short edges, leaving a ⅝" (1.5cm) gap ⅝" (1.5cm) below the long upper edge and a 2½" (6.5cm) gap ¾" (2cm) above the long lower edge. Press the seam open. Stitch the tub lining to the base lining in the same way as the interfaced outer tub (step 2).

5. **Insert the lining.** Slip the outer tub into the lining with right sides facing, matching the seams and upper raw edge. If you can remove the bed of the sewing machine, do so

and slip the tub over the arm of the machine. Stitch the upper edge. Refer to the grading (layering) seam allowances technique (page 12) to trim the seam allowance.

6. **Finish the lining.** Turn the tub right side out through the large gap in the lining. Adjust the seam allowances toward the lining. Slipstitch the large gap closed. Press the lining to the inside ¾" (2cm) above the seam.

7. **Add the boning.** Topstitch just above the seam, then close to the upper pressed edge to form a channel. Insert plastic boning through the small gap in the channel, allowing the ends to overlap inside the channel. Lift the loop and catch it securely to the back of the channel with a few stitches.

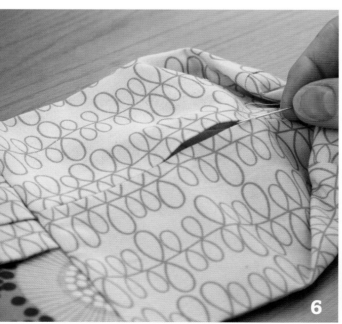

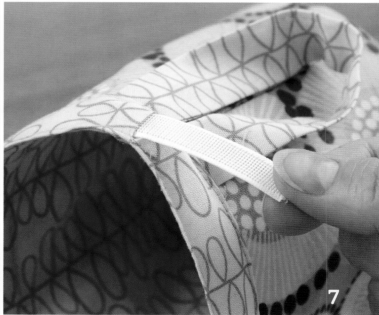

Tablet Sleeve

Decorate this practical tablet case with a stem of appliquéd and embroidered leaves. The case is padded and stiffened with interfacing and has a hook and loop fastener to keep its contents secure.

Materials

- 14" x 6" (35 x 15cm) rectangle of printed cotton fabric
- 16" x 14" (40 x 35cm) rectangle of striped cotton fabric, stripes parallel with short edges
- 20" x 4" (50 x 10cm) rectangle of lightweight iron-on interfacing
- 20" x 14" (50 x 35cm) rectangle of lightweight batting (wadding)
- 20" x 14" (50 x 35cm) rectangle medium-weight sew-in interfacing
- 20" x 16" (50 x 40cm) rectangle of plain cotton fabric
- Embroidery floss to match plain fabric
- 4" (10cm) of ¾" (2cm)-wide sew-on hook and loop tape

Cutting Out

- Find the leaf template for the tablet sleeve on page 94.
- Cut one 12" x 3¾" (30 x 10cm) rectangle for the band from printed fabric.
- Cut one 12" x 6" (30 x 15cm) rectangle for the front and one 12" x 9" (30 x 23cm) rectangle for the back from striped fabric, with the stripes parallel with the short edges.
- Cut two 12" x 9" (30 x 23cm) rectangles from batting (wadding), medium-weight sew-in interfacing, and plain fabric for the linings.
- Cut ten leaves from plain fabric and lightweight iron-on interfacing.

Tip

The appliquéd leaves would look great on other home accessories too, such as a cushion or the toiletry bag on page 82.

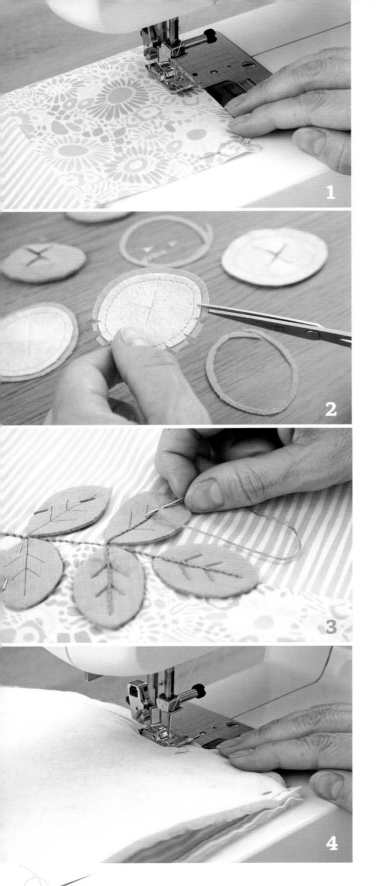

Making the tablet sleeve

1. **Start the front.** Pin and stitch the long left-hand edge of the band to the long right-hand edge of the front with right sides facing, using a ⅜" (1cm) seam allowance. Press the seam open.

2. **Make the leaves.** Press the interfacing leaves to the wrong side of the fabric leaves. Refer to the template to cut a cross along the dotted lines on five leaves. With right sides facing, pin each leaf with a cross to a leaf without a cross. Stitch the outer edges, using a ¼" (6mm) seam allowance. Refer to the grading (layering) seam allowances technique (page 12) to grade the seam allowance. Snip the curves and turn right side out. Press the leaves.

3. **Embroider the leaves.** Separate and use three strands of embroidery floss to embroider a stem stitch along the front seam, finishing 4¼" (10.5cm) below the upper edge. To embroider a stem stitch, bring the needle to the right side. Keeping the thread below the line, insert the needle forward ⅛" (3mm) along the line, bring the needle out on the line in the middle of the stitch, pull the thread through, and continue along the line. Draw a central line and veins on the right side of the leaves with an air-erasable pen. Refer to the photo to pin the leaves to the front piece from step 1. Embroider a stem stitch along the center lines. Embroider the veins with straight stitches. Do all leaf embroidery through the front of the sleeve, securing the leaves to the sleeve.

4. **Assemble the layers.** In two sets, place batting (wadding) on the sew-in interfacing pieces. Pin the front and back, right side up, on top of each set, then baste (tack) the outer edges. Pin the front and back together with right sides facing. Stitch the outer edges, using a ⅜" (1cm) seam allowance and leaving the short upper edge open. Clip the corners. Press the seam open by running the tip of the iron along the seam to avoid flattening the batting (wadding). Turn the case right side out.

5. **Add the closures.** Pin each hook and loop tape section on the right side of the linings, centered

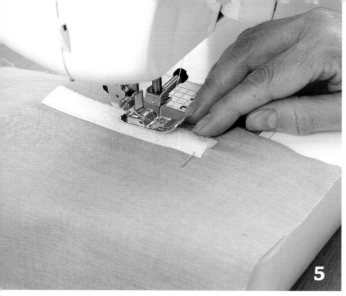

⅝" (1.5cm) below the short upper edge. Stitch close to the outer edges.

6. **Make the lining.** Press the hook and loop sections together. Using a ⅜" (1cm) seam allowance, pin and stitch the outer edges of the linings together, leaving the upper edge open and a 6" (15cm) gap in one long edge. Clip the corners and press the seam open.

7. **Assemble the case.** Slip the case into the lining with right sides together and matching the seams. If possible, take the bed off the sewing machine and slip the case and lining over the arm. Stitch the upper edge, using a ⅜" (1cm) seam allowance. Carefully trim away the batting (wadding) in the seam allowance.

8. **Finish the case.** Turn the case right side out through the gap in the lining. Slipstitch the gap closed. Press the lining to the inside along the upper edge. Pin the case and lining together at the upper edge, matching the seams. Slip the case back over the arm of the sewing machine if possible. Topstitch 1¼" (3cm) below the upper edge.

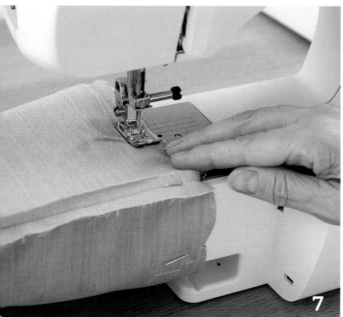

Toiletry Bag

This travel-size bag would make a lovely "bon voyage" gift. It is lightly padded to protect the contents and the corners are stitched to form a gusset that allows the bag to stand upright.

Materials

- 8" x 8" (20 x 20cm) square of printed cotton fabric (fabric A)
- 16" x 8" (40 x 20cm) rectangle of printed cotton fabric (fabric B)
- 20" x 8" (50 x 20cm) rectangle of lightweight white cotton fabric
- 20" x 8" (50 x 20cm) rectangle of lightweight batting (wadding)
- 20" x 8" (50 x 20cm) rectangle of plain cotton fabric
- 20" (50cm) of ⅝" (1.5cm)-wide ribbon
- 7" (18cm) zipper

Cutting Out

- Cut two 7" x 3¼" (18 x 8cm) rectangles for the bag from fabric A.
- Cut two 7" x 6¼" (18 x 16cm) rectangles for the bag and two 2" x 1" (5 x 2.5cm) rectangles for the zipper end covers from fabric B.
- Cut two 8¾" x 7" (22 x 18cm) rectangles of batting (wadding), lightweight white cotton fabric, and plain fabric for the lining.

Tip

To make a waterproof lining, use shower curtain fabric and stitch with a Teflon foot on the sewing machine. Don't press waterproof fabric—instead, stitch a ⅜" (1cm) hem on the upper edge in step 6.

Making the toiletry bag

1. **Make the outside.** With right sides facing, stitch each fabric A bag to a fabric B bag along one long edge, using a ⅜" (1cm) seam allowance. Press the seams open. Cut two 7" (18cm) lengths of ribbon. With right sides facing up, pin the ribbon along the seams with the seams centered. Stitch close to the long edges of the ribbon. Place the batting (wadding) on the lightweight fabric rectangles, then place the printed bags right side up on top. Smooth the fabrics out from the center and pin the layers together. Baste (tack) around the outer edges.

2. **Prepare the zipper.** Press under ⅜" (1cm) on the short edges of the zipper end covers. Press the covers in half parallel with the pressed edges with wrong sides facing. Trim an equal amount off each end of the zipper to make the overall length 7¾" (19.5cm). Slightly open the zipper. Slip each end of the zipper into a zipper end cover, with the raw edges of the covers level with the long edges of the zipper. Baste (tack) in place through all the layers.

3. **Attach the zipper.** With the zipper centered and right sides facing, pin one long edge of the zipper to the upper long edge of one bag side. Use a zipper foot to stitch in place, using a ⅜" (1cm) seam allowance. Repeat to stitch the other long edge of the zipper to the other bag side. Press the bags away from the zipper. Topstitch close to the zipper teeth.

4. **Assemble the outside.** Open the zipper. Pin the bags together with right sides facing. Stitch the raw edges, using a ⅜" (1cm) seam allowance. Press the seam open by running the tip of the iron along the seam to avoid flattening the batting (wadding).

5. **Form the base.** Fold one lower corner with right sides together, matching the seams. Mark a line across the corner with a row of pins at right angles to the seam

1" (2.5cm) from the corner. Stitch along the pinned line; the seam will be 2" (5cm) long. Cut off the corner, leaving a ⅜" (1cm) seam allowance. Repeat on the other lower corner.

6. **Make the lining.** Press under ⅜" (1cm) on the long upper edges of the linings. With right sides facing, pin and stitch the linings together along the raw edges, using a ⅜" (1cm) seam allowance. Press the seam open. Repeat step 5 to stitch across the corners and trim the seams.

7. **Insert the lining.** Turn the lining right side out. Insert the bag into the lining, matching the seams. Pin and slipstitch the pressed edges of the lining around the zipper and upper corners of the bag. Turn the bag right side out.

8. **Add the zipper pull.** Press the remaining ribbon lengthwise in half. Insert the ribbon through the hole in the zipper pull. Adjust the ribbon until the ends are level. Stitch across the ribbon, then trim the ends diagonally.

Tote Bag

This bag is a great size and its handles are long enough to wear on a shoulder, making it a very handy accessory on any trip. To give it a jaunty twist, make the handles in a bright, contrasting color.

Materials

- 30" x 20" (75 x 50cm) of home-décor-weight printed cotton fabric, short edges parallel with selvage
- 8" (20cm) of 44" (112cm)-wide plain cotton fabric
- 8" (20cm) of 36" (90cm)-wide lightweight iron-on interfacing
- 9" (23cm) diameter dinner plate

Cutting Out

- Cut two 16" x 14½" (40 x 37cm) rectangles for the bag from printed fabric.
- Cut two 25½" x 4" (60 x 10cm) strips for the handles from plain fabric.
- Cut two 24¾" x 3¼" (58 x 8cm) strips from iron-on interfacing.

Making the tote bag

1. **Cut the bag shape.** Place a 9" (23cm) diameter plate on the lower corner of one bag piece. Use a pencil to draw around the curve that lies within the corner. Remove the plate. Fold the bag lengthwise in half. Pin the layers together close to the curve. Cut the bag along the curved line to curve both corners on the lower edge. Repeat on the other bag piece. Open out the bags. Finish (neaten) the long side and short lower edges with a zigzag stitch or pinking shears.

2. **Start the handles.** Press the interfacing strips centrally to the wrong side of the fabric handles. Press the long edges of the fabric over the interfacing. Press the handles lengthwise in half with wrong sides facing. Pin the pressed edges together.

3. **Continue the handles.** Topstitch close to the long pressed edges. Press under ⅜" (1cm) on the ends of the handles and snip diagonally across the corners.

4. **Attach the handles.** With right sides facing up, pin the ends of one handle to one bag 3⅛" (8cm) in from the side edges and 4¼" (11cm) below the upper edge. At each end, stitch close to the edges and across the handle, forming a square, then stitch a cross formation in the center of the square. Repeat on the other bag.

5. **Assemble the halves.** Pin the bags together with right sides facing. Stitch the outer edges, using a ⅝" (1.5cm) seam allowance and leaving the upper edge open. Press the seam open.

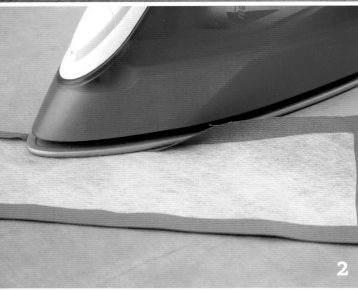

4

5

6. **Finish the bag.** Slip the bag over a sleeve board or the end of the ironing board. Press under ⅜" (1cm), then 1¼" (3cm) on the upper edge to form a hem. Pin the hem in position. Turn the bag right side out. On the right side, topstitch 1" (2.5cm) below the upper pressed edge to secure the hem.

Tip

Take care not to accidentally stitch the handles when topstitching the hem.

6

Wall Organizer

Keep your odds and ends sorted in this neat organizer that can be hung on a door or a wall. The edges are finished with bias binding. Have fun picking complementary (or contrasting!) fabrics.

Materials

- 14" x 8" (35 x 20cm) rectangle of printed cotton fabric (fabric A)
- 18" (45cm) of 36" (90cm)-wide medium-weight sew-in interfacing
- 18" (45cm) of 44" (112cm)-wide plain cotton fabric
- 16" x 16" (40 x 40cm) square of printed cotton fabric (fabric B)
- 2¾ yd. (2.5m) of 1" (2.5cm)-wide bias binding
- 22" (55cm) of ½" (1.2cm)-wide bias binding
- Two 1" (2.5cm) D-rings

Cutting Out

- Find the wall organizer templates on pages 100 and 101.
- Cut two small pockets, right side up, from fabric A and sew-in interfacing.
- Cut one medium pocket, right side up, and one large pocket on the fold from fabric B and sew-in interfacing.
- Cut two small pockets, wrong side up, one medium pocket, wrong side up, one large pocket on the fold, and two 16½" x 12" (42 x 30cm) rectangles for the organizer from plain fabric.
- Cut one 16½" x 12" (42 x 30cm) rectangle for the organizer from sew-in interfacing.

Tip

Keep the binding taut when pinning it to the curved edge of the pockets so that the binding won't pucker when folded over the concave curve.

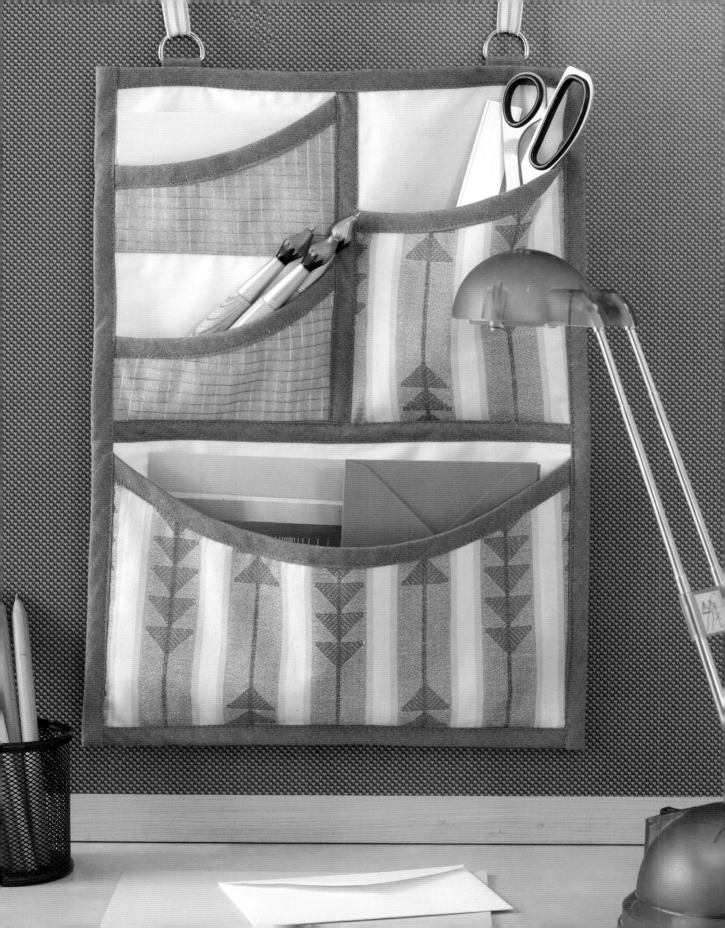

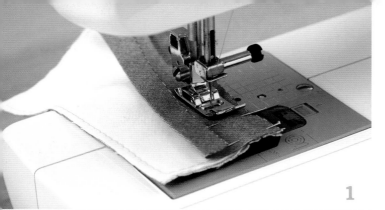

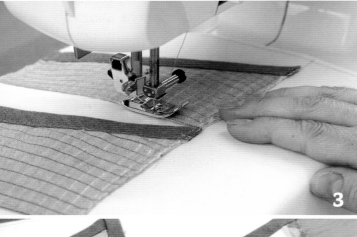

Making the organizer

1. **Start the pockets.** Pin and baste (tack) the pocket interfacing between the printed and plain pockets with the right sides facing out. Refer to step 1 of the single-fold binding technique (page 14) to stitch 1" (2.5cm)-wide binding to the curved edge on the plain side of the pockets, then turn the binding over the raw edge, just covering the seam, and pin in place. Stitch close to the pressed edge of the binding.

2. **Finish the pockets.** Cut the ends of the binding level with the side edges of the pockets. Press under ¼" (6mm) on the long lower edge of one small pocket.

3. **Attach the small pockets.** Pin and baste (tack) the organizer interfacing between the fabric organizers with the right sides facing out. Use a sharp #2 (HB) pencil to draw a horizontal line across the organizer 7¾" (19.5cm) above the short lower edge, and a vertical line parallel with the long edges along the center from the upper short edge to the horizontal line. With right sides facing up, pin and baste (tack) the small pockets to the left-hand half, with the tip of the pocket that has the pressed edge ½" (1.2cm) below the short upper edge of the organizer, and matching the raw edges of the pockets to the left-hand side edge and drawn lines. Topstitch close to the pressed edge.

4. **Attach the medium pocket.** With right sides facing up, pin and baste (tack) the medium pocket to the right-hand half of the organizer, matching the raw edges of the pocket to the drawn lines and right-hand raw edge of the organizer. Pin ½" (1.2cm)-wide bias binding over the drawn vertical line, covering the raw edges, with the vertical line centered. Cut the binding level with the horizontal line. Baste (tack) in place. Stitch close to both long edges of the binding.

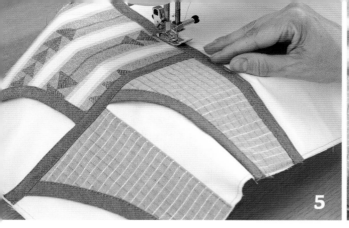

5. **Bind the bottoms of the pockets.** With the horizontal line centered, pin and baste (tack) ½" (1.2cm)-wide bias binding over the horizontal line, covering the lower raw edges of the pockets. Cut the binding level with the side edges. Stitch close to both long edges of the binding.

6. **Attach the large pocket.** With right sides facing up, pin and baste (tack) the large pocket to the bottom of the organizer, matching the raw edges. Refer to step 1 of the single-fold binding technique (page 14) to stitch 1" (2.5cm)-wide bias binding to the lower edge on the underside of the organizer. Cut the binding level with the side edges. Turn the binding over the raw edge, just covering the seam, and pin in place. Stitch close to the pressed edge. Repeat to bind the upper edge of the organizer.

7. **Bind the side edges.** Refer to step 1 of the single-fold binding technique (page 14) to

pin and stitch 1" (2.5cm)-wide bias bindings to the long edges on the underside of the organizer with ⅜" (1cm) of the binding extending at each end. Lightly press the binding away from the organizer. Fold the ends of the binding over the short edges of the organizer and hand sew in place. Turn the bindings over the raw edges, just covering the seam, and pin in place. Stitch close to the pressed edges.

8. **Add the loops.** Cut two 2" (5cm) lengths of 1" (2.5cm)-wide bias binding for the hanging loops. Slip each loop through a D-ring and pin the raw edges together. Baste (tack) the hanging loops under the upper edge 1½" (4cm) in from the long side edges, with the D-ring just above the upper edge of the organizer. On the right side, stitch just below the binding, stitching back and forth to secure the hanging loops in place.

Templates

Some of the projects in this book refer to templates. Trace the templates onto tracing paper or enlarge them on a photocopier as indicated. Remember to transfer any grain lines, fold lines, and other useful information.

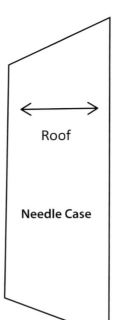

Roof

Needle Case

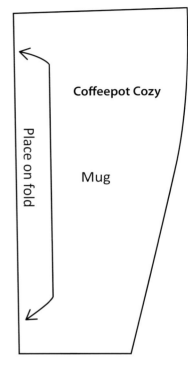

Coffeepot Cozy

Place on fold

Mug

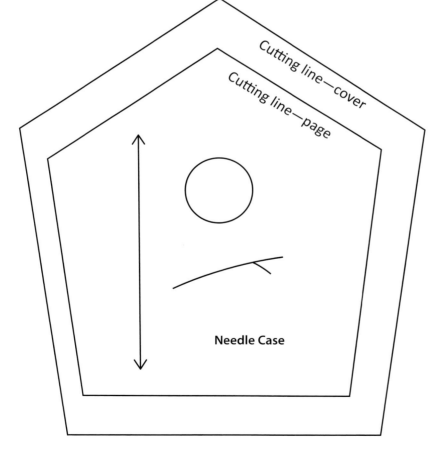

Cutting line—cover

Cutting line—page

Needle Case

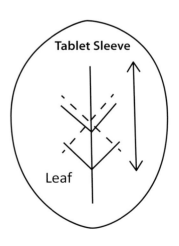

Tablet Sleeve

Leaf

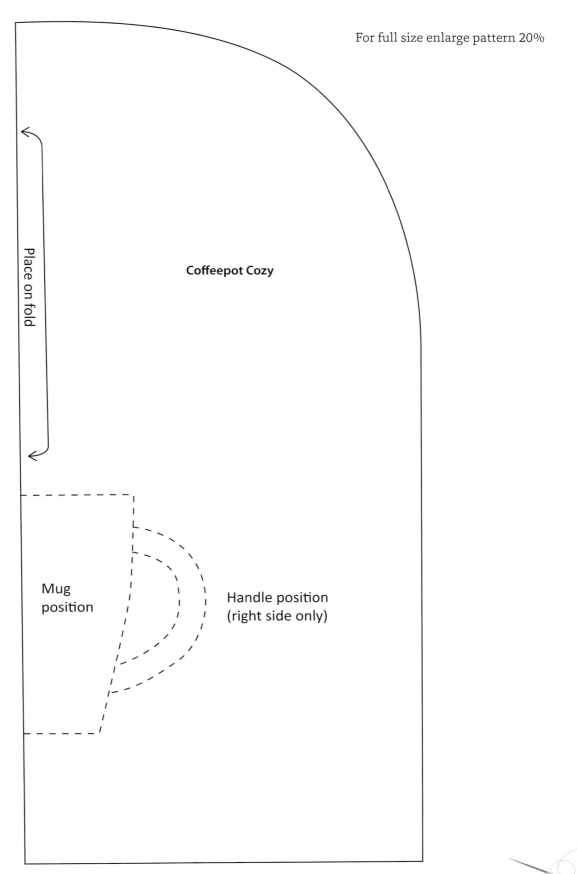

For full size enlarge pattern 20%

Place on fold

Coffeepot Cozy

Mug
position

Handle position
(right side only)

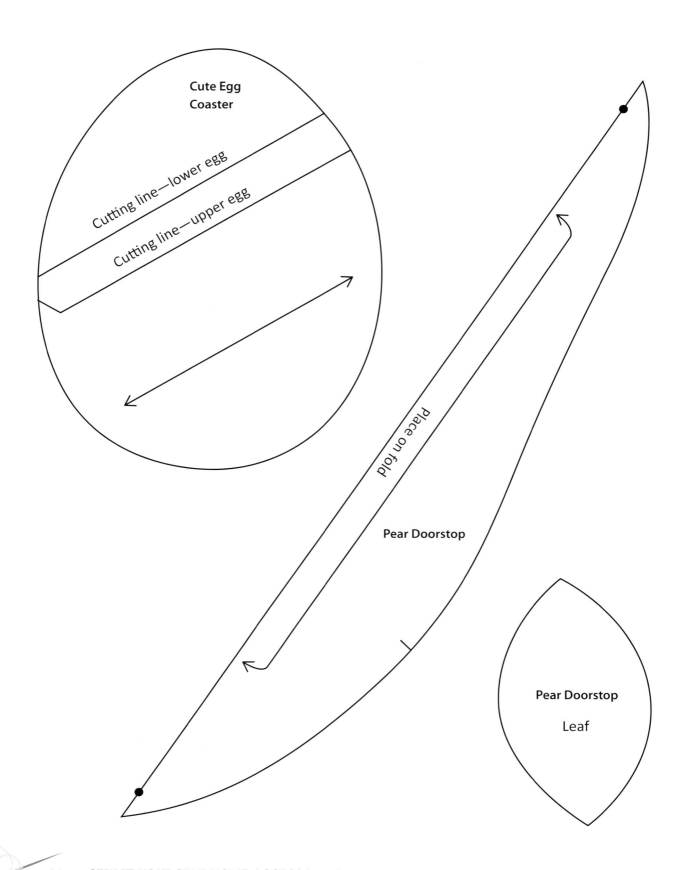

Cute Egg Coaster

Cutting line—lower egg

Cutting line—upper egg

place on fold

Pear Doorstop

Pear Doorstop

Leaf

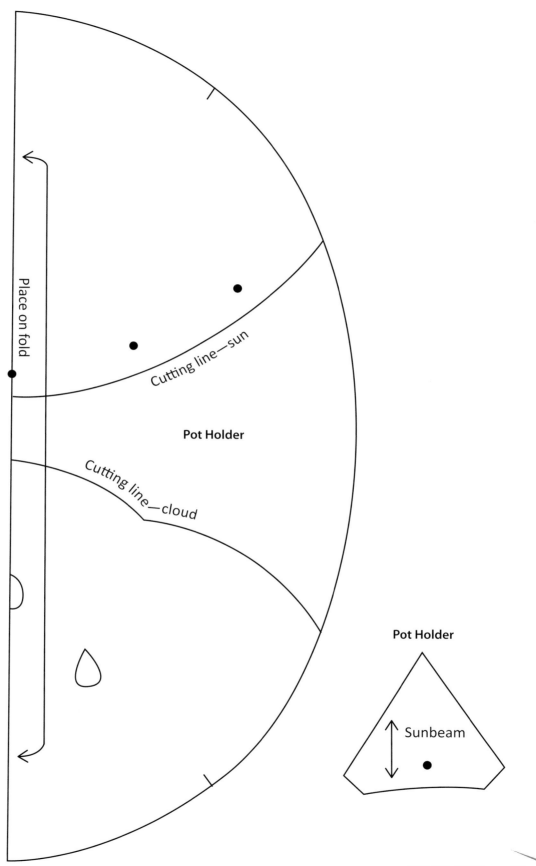

Place on fold

Cutting line—sun

Pot Holder

Cutting line—cloud

Pot Holder

Sunbeam

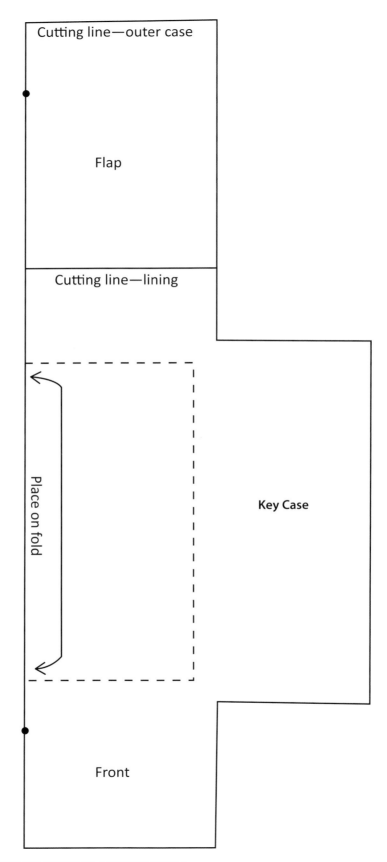

Cutting line—outer case

Flap

Cutting line—lining

Place on fold

Key Case

Front

For full size enlarge pattern 20%

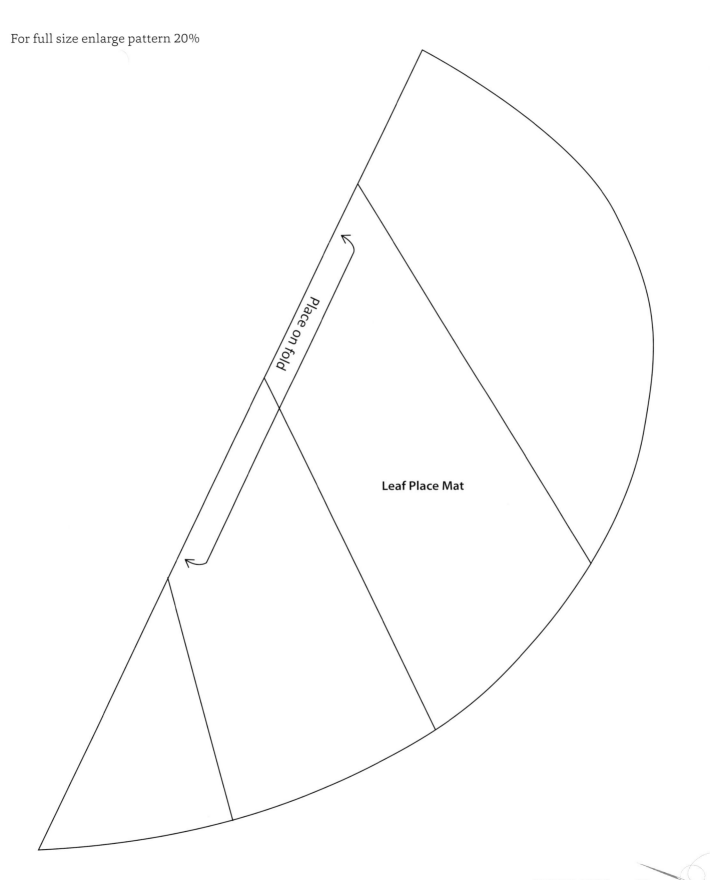

Place on fold

Leaf Place Mat

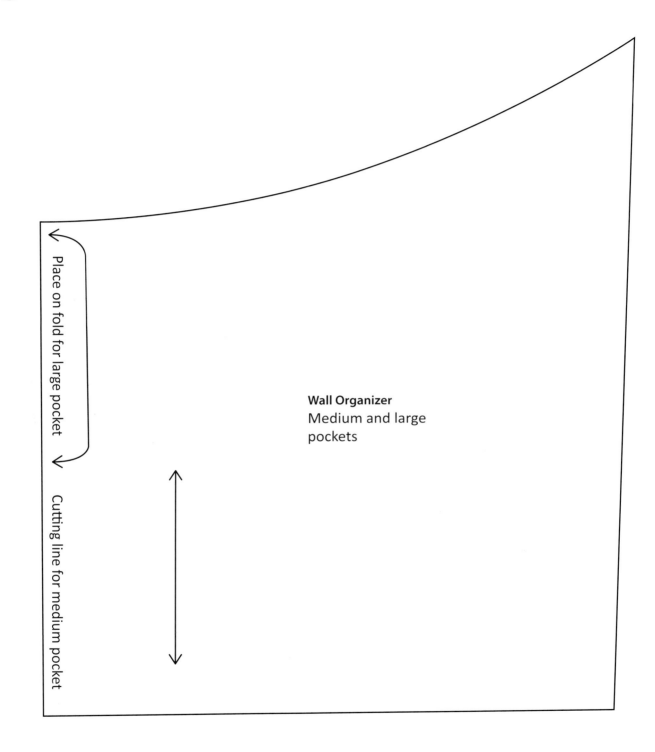

Place on fold for large pocket

Cutting line for medium pocket

Wall Organizer
Medium and large
pockets

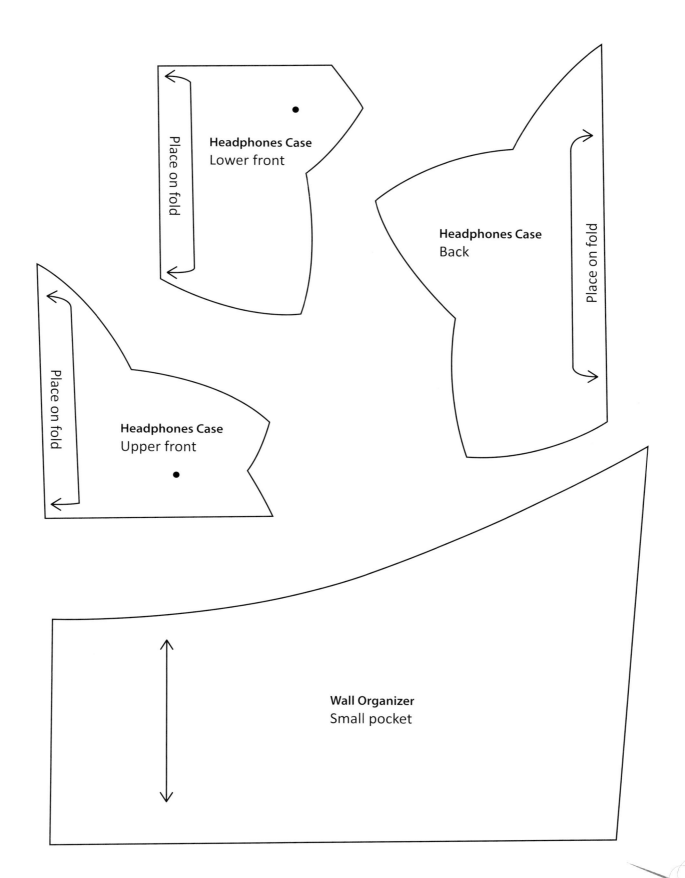

Headphones Case
Lower front

Place on fold

Headphones Case
Back

Place on fold

Place on fold

Headphones Case
Upper front

Wall Organizer
Small pocket

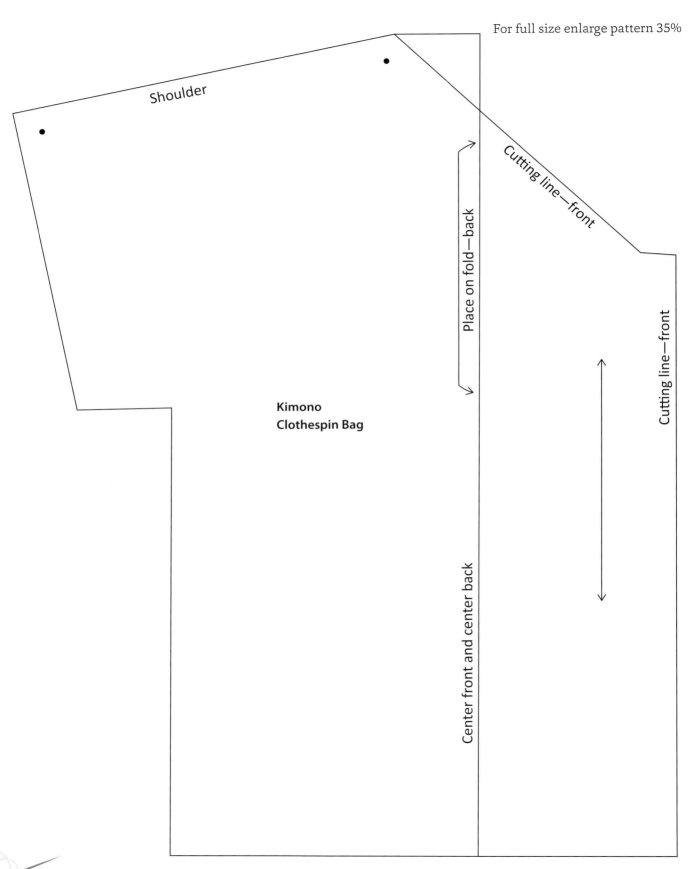

For full size enlarge pattern 35%

Shoulder

Cutting line—front

Cutting line—front

Place on fold—back

Kimono
Clothespin Bag

Center front and center back

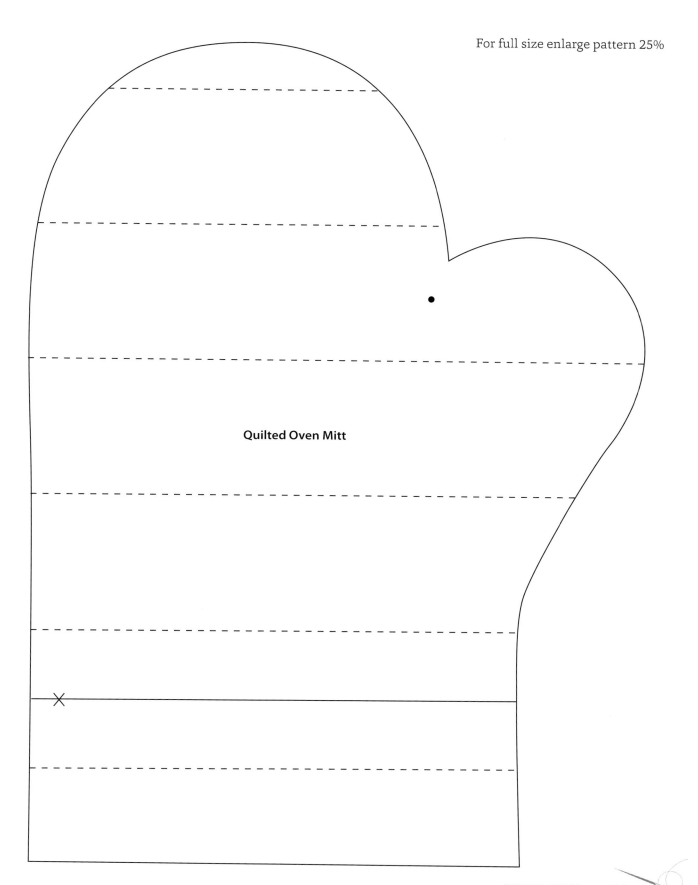

For full size enlarge pattern 25%

Quilted Oven Mitt

Index

Note: Page numbers in *italics* indicate projects/templates.